CLASS OF 92

CLASS OF 92

THE OFFICIAL STORY OF THE TEAM
THAT TRANSFORMED UNITED

IAN MARSHALL

SIMON &
SCHUSTER

London · New York · Sydney · Toronto · New Delhi

A CBS COMPANY

First published in Great Britain by Simon & Schuster UK Ltd, 2012
A CBS COMPANY

Copyright © Manchester United Football Club Limited, 2012

The right of Ian Marshall to be identified as author of this work
has been asserted by him in accordance with sections 77 and
78 of the Copyright, Designs and Patents Act, 1988.

1 3 5 7 9 10 8 6 4 2

Simon & Schuster UK Ltd
1st Floor
222 Gray's Inn Road
London
WC1X 8HB

www.simonandschuster.co.uk

Simon & Schuster Australia, Sydney
Simon & Schuster India, New Delhi

A CIP catalogue record for this book
is available from the British Library

Hardback ISBN 978-1-47110-263-9
TPB ISBN 978-1-47111-064-1

Typeset by M Rules
Printed and bound by CPI Group (UK) Ltd, Croydon, CR0 4YY

To Kiri and Sophia
The Class of 2004 and 2006

Contents

Introduction

'They've got to be in love with football.'

Paul McGuinness

The date is Wednesday 18 January 2012, and a crowd of 993 has come out to Altrincham's Moss Lane ground to watch a game of football. It is pretty much an average attendance for the Robins. But Altrincham aren't playing. Instead, it's a bunch of teenagers in action. And one of the teams comes into the match with an astonishing pedigree from years gone by. Manchester United's Youth Cup side of 2011–12 are the keepers of a flame that dates back to the Busby Babes (Bobby Charlton and Duncan Edwards among them), through George Best and on to 'Fergie's Fledglings', the Class of 92 that featured some of the greatest players of the modern era. That's some heritage to live up to.

United's opponents tonight are Derby County, conquerors of Arsenal in the previous round, and it is the visitors who gain the early momentum. After 20 minutes, it is the young

Rams (looking anything but lambs to the slaughter) who take the lead when Kane Richards scores past Liam Jacob. For a brief moment, the Reds look uncertain and could have conceded another goal within seconds. But soon their training kicks in, they begin to pass the ball around and the balance of the tie begins to shift.

The game has become a war of attrition. There seems little space for anyone to express themselves, with the midfield congested; the heavy pitch ensures it is hard to create any room for expansive play. Then, with five minutes remaining in the first half, Jack Barmby's run at the defence results in his shot looping up into the air and, when the Derby keeper Mats Mørch fails to hold on to the ball, it lands at Barmby's feet and he slots it home for the equaliser. This is more like it.

One of the most striking things about youth football, for those who are used to seeing the seniors in action, is that it is truly a family experience – and Barmby, of course, personifies this. His father, Nick (currently managing his home-town club Hull City), played for Tottenham in the FA Youth Cup semi-final 20 years ago, losing out to United's famed Class of 92. Not only did Barmby senior lose, he was also sent off in that game. Despite that setback, three years later he was playing for England.

The family element is also present on the touchline, where the team's manager is Paul McGuinness, son of Wilf (who won the Youth Cup with United on three occasions as a player, between 1954 and 1956). The link between the McGuinness family and the Youth Cup thus extends back to all but the first year it was contested. Paul recalls his father talking about the Youth Cup and how important it was in creating the Busby Babes – 'I grew up with it,' he says. Indeed, he too came through the youth system at Old Trafford, so has experienced what it is like at first hand himself.

In the end, Paul's playing career did not take off, so he got his coaching badges, went to university to study PE and Sports Science, and by the age of 26 was back at United as the educational welfare officer, making sure the youngsters coming through the School of Excellence and the Academy did not neglect their studies. For some, a day away from training was a good break.

McGuinness has been in charge of the Youth Cup side for six or seven years now. He is grateful to have the Class of 92 as examples to hold before his players, and his advice to them is, 'They've got to be in love with football.' His other key point is that this is a vital time for them when they must concentrate and work hard: 'It's normal for lads of fifteen, sixteen and seventeen to switch off occasionally, but we're not looking for normal.'

Sitting just behind McGuinness is the father of the modern United, the man who ensures that it remains a family club, despite also being a major world-famous corporate brand valued at around £1.5 billion: Sir Alex Ferguson. He is here, watching over his kids as he has done for more than 25 years since he took charge of the club. No doubt he would like to catch up with Sir Matt Busby's achievement of winning this trophy six times; currently he's on four.

But, perhaps above all, the family atmosphere is present in the stands. Among the crowd are the parents of the players, families taking young kids to have an early taste of going to a football match in a safe environment (there's no swearing to be heard, nor any obscene chants). Behind me, a father explains to his son some of the intricacies of what is happening on the pitch. It's a school night, but the game will be over before nine, so it doesn't matter that he's here.

There are also many people like Keith Topping here: he has been a regular at youth-team football matches for almost 30 years, and he can recall watching the United youth sides of the 1980s and 1990s. He is in no doubt that it was the Class of 92 who were the best he's ever seen at this level. He comes along because of the special atmosphere you get when Academy side is in action. There's just something special about it, he says. Robbie Savage, a graduate of the Class of 92, now goes to watch his son play at the United Academy and sees some of the same faces who were there when he was starting out. It is a world where hope truly does spring eternal.

After the interval, United increasingly begin to take a grip on the tie. The minibus-load of Derby supporters, who spent much of the first half singing for their players, have now gone much quieter in the stand opposite. On the hour mark, United captain Luke McCullough, who has played much of the game carrying a knock, finally makes way; one or two others begin to cramp up and tire – the pitch is having its effect. With ten minutes remaining, Adnan Januzaj, the Belgium-born midfielder who will not be 17 until next month, is brought down in the box by Rhys Sharpe – it's a clear penalty. Barmby steps up and slots the ball into the bottom left-hand corner to give United a 2–1 lead, and there's even a chance to give a run-out to school-boys Nicolas Ioannou, Louis Rowley and James Wilson. The

Reds duly hold on to go through to meet Swansea in the fifth round for a place in the quarter-finals. The majority of the crowd spill out of the ground happy with the result and discussing what they have just seen.

Although the 2012 crop is a young side, the senior players keep a close watch on those coming through. Rio Ferdinand comments: 'I've seen them train and watched a few games and we've got a lot of young but very talented players this year. Who knows? We may have to wait, but they may surprise and might come out and just batter every team they play against, which I hope they do. But you'll probably see the best of this team next season in terms of physical prowess and development . . . I think they'll do well this year and surprise a few people and probably a few people at the club, too.'

Any football match will provide talking points, but the Youth Cup is different. The focus of people's discussions isn't on a controversial refereeing decision or the form of a struggling star player: it's about the game and its participants; it's about hope for the future. One of the joys of watching Academy in action – the reason why so many like Keith Topping keep coming to see them – is that an unusual sense of optimism reigns. Will Barmby go on to follow in his father's footsteps and reach the top? Centre-forward Gyliano van Velzen is a very pacey striker who makes a number of great runs in the channels – does he remind you of Andrew Cole? Right-back Donald Love keeps bombing down the wing on the overlap, just like Gary Neville did for so many years. Local boy Tyler Blackett looks strong and assured in defence, capable of playing both at left-back or centre-back – can he be the next local lad to make it through to the first team, the path most recently taken by Danny Welbeck?

There are so many questions and so many hopes wrapped up in watching these lads of 16 and 17 as they try to make the next step up to adult football. In the back of their minds, they know what awaits them if they have the ability, work very hard and avoid any injuries or distractions that might interrupt their progress. They only have to look at the first team where, 20 years on from their own Youth Cup exploits, Giggs and Scholes are still turning out for United, still wanting to keep playing for the best club in the world and still looking to win more honours. Still working. That's what the future could hold. Will the 993 of us who saw United win the fourth round of the FA Youth Cup on 18 January 2012 be able to look back in years to come and say 'I was there' when one of them was taking his first steps to greatness? We can but hope. And it is that sense of hope that makes the Youth Cup such a special tournament.

This book tells the story of a remarkable group of young players. For so many of United's Class of 92, their hopes and dreams came true. They not only won the FA Youth Cup that year, but many of them went on to have spectacular careers in the game. In the process, they were (and in two cases remain) instrumental in bringing an unprecedented amount of success to Manchester United. Between them, they won 48 Premier League title medals at United; only five players in United's history have made more than 600 appearances for the Reds in their careers – three of them emerged from that youth team. Perhaps surprisingly to modern eyes,

Introduction

Paul Scholes did not appear at all during the Youth Cup campaign of 1991–92, but (along with Phil Neville) he played a part in the attempted defence of the trophy the following year. Both men are therefore a part of the Class of 92.

But this book is about more than just the extraordinary tale of how that group of players came to win the 1992 Youth Cup 20 years ago. It also looks at why this tournament has such a strong place in the hearts of United fans, for no other club has won it as often. So many times United's history, success in the Youth Cup has been followed by triumph at senior level, as the players make the step up to the next stage. United's track record for bringing in new blood to the first team is surely unique.

This belief in the potential of youth has guided the club's two greatest managers – Sir Matt Busby and Sir Alex Ferguson – and has become part of United's DNA. As Busby once said: 'If you want football's finest fruit, then you grow your own.' Ferguson echoed his predecessor's thoughts by calling the youth system United's 'lifeblood'. As former youth-team manager Eric Harrison explained, the fans understand it too: 'They certainly wouldn't accept it if we had a team full of foreigners ... because they'd be saying where's the young players, where's the kids out of the youth team? Where are they? They want it, we want it and long may that continue.'

However, though the story of the Class of 92 is one of youth vindicated and triumphant, it is not as simple as that. It never is with youth football. For some, success never came on the football pitch, while for others opportunities had to be sought away from Old Trafford. And this uncertainty and human drama is what draws us all in: we don't know when we see these teenagers in action how their story will develop. Anything can happen. And, after all, isn't that why we watch football: because we never know what will happen next?

One of United's current stars, Rio Ferdinand, who got to the Youth Cup final in 1996 with West Ham United, gives a player's perspective on it all: 'I think it's a great tournament as you get to play at stadiums and get a real feel of what it's like to play in big games as a young player . . . It can be a launching pad for many careers. We've seen, over the years, players have gone on from doing well in the FA Youth Cup to becoming regulars in the first teams, so it's a great opportunity for them.'

It's also a great opportunity for us as fans, too. But to understand why United's love affair with the FA Youth Cup is so strong, we have to go back to the beginning, when it all started in the 'Austerity Britain' of 60 years ago.

1

Gentlemen Ferrets and the Busby Legacy

'If you want football's finest fruit, then you grow your own.'

Sir Matt Busby

Nothing excites a football fan like the sight of a bright young prospect showing dazzling skills and playing with the freedom of youth. This is why many truly dedicated supporters will not just watch the first team at their club, but also the junior teams. However, the route taken from youth football to the senior sides has changed over the years, and the path that takes them there today is a surprisingly recent creation.

As the Second World War drew to a close, the Football Association not only recognised the appeal of junior football among fans, but also realised they had the makings of a serious problem. There had been no 'proper' league football since 1939, which meant many of the established players from the 1930s would no longer be available to play – lost to the game because of age, injury or tragically killed during the conflict. Bringing through young players as quickly as possible would be vital if football was to thrive once peace was restored, as they would help make up the numbers and provide a new group of heroes to replace the ones who had gone before.

Because of this, as early as 1944–45 the sport's ruling body initiated the FA County Youth Challenge Cup, to try to give junior football in England a proper structure. But this competition struggled to establish itself, because it wasn't linked to the Football League clubs. The FA soon realised it had to work with the professional clubs if it was to build a successful tournament, rather than relying on its own regional structures to do the job. After all, a player's future career depended on the clubs not the counties.

The man who saw the nature of the problem was Sir Stanley Rous, the secretary of the FA from 1934 to 1962, and one of the game's most influential and forward-thinking administrators. The first official mention of what was to become the FA Youth Challenge Cup came in an FA meeting on 2 May 1952. The minutes note: 'The Council received a report that two meetings were held on 4 February and 24 March 1952 to explore the possibilities of organising a National Youth Competition under the aegis of The Football Association on a knock-out regional basis to be open to Clubs in membership with The Football Association.' It was agreed that the competition should be limited to those aged between 15 and 18 on 1 September of the season concerned.

As the minutes noted, earlier in 1952 Rous had met with the Northern Intermediate League Management Committee and representatives of interested Football League clubs to garner support for his initiative. From there, things moved forward quickly. The FA committee responsible for running the inaugural competition met for the first time at FA head-quarters in Lancaster Gate, London, on 6 August, and reported that 93 clubs had decided to enter the cup, and among them was Manchester United.

It may not seem much now, but in fact this was an enor-mous achievement for Rous, who was trying to bring the organisation into the modern era. Where previously the amateur-led counties had played a pivotal role in the FA, he recognised that the professional clubs were the ones who could really drive things forward.

The scale of the challenges he faced can be gathered by the way the first ever England manager, Walter Winterbottom, was recruited. Originally he was appointed in 1946 to work as the FA's director of coaching. Having brought in his man, Rous subsequently added the role of manager of the England team to his list of tasks. It seems strange to the modern eye that the job of England manager could ever be seen as almost an afterthought, but it was in fact a hugely controversial step – albeit an obvious one.

Many on the FA committee profoundly disagreed with this appointment, as the job of selecting the England side had previously been carried out by alternating FA Council mem-bers, and they were reluctant to lose this power. But if there was any doubt that the way the game in England was run was inadequate, the evidence soon became overwhelming. After England rejoined FIFA, and then got taught a painful lesson in the 1950 World Cup, it was clear that everything the FA did needed to be more professional, both at international and at youth level. The FA Youth Cup was part of its response to this challenge.

It was no surprise that United were keen to take part in this new competition, as they had been one of the first to develop a strong youth policy, realising that (if nothing else) it was a cheap way of recruiting new players. Contrary to popular belief, it wasn't Matt Busby who initiated United's successful youth programme, but club chairman James Gibson in the 1930s. Early in the 1930s, the club ran an 'A' side, coached by Lal Hilditch, but it wasn't until towards the end of the decade that the arrangement became more formalised. At the time, most clubs were not doing anything like this, though Wolverhampton Wanderers under Major Frank Buckley were the pioneers, setting up their youth system in 1927.

The Manchester United Junior Athletic Club (MUJAC) was set up just before the war to ensure the best young players in the Manchester area made their way to Old Trafford rather than to local rivals City, or indeed to any other club. MUJAC was first mentioned in the United board minutes on 22 February 1938 and the aim was stated as 'cultivating young players after they leave school'.

Although the men most closely involved in the process were Gibson, club secretary Walter Crickmer and chief scout Louis Rocca, the crucial part to making it work in practice was a committee of teachers and instructors from Manchester University. They helped solidify the links between the club and the schools. With Louis Rocca in charge of the scouting network, United were able to recruit some notable young talents in the years before the outbreak of war, most famously defender Johnny Carey, who was brought over from Ireland, but also local boy John Aston, winger Charlie Mitten, Johnny Morris and Salford-born forward Stan Pearson. All of them were part of the United set-up that Busby inherited when he took up his post as manager of the club in October 1945, and they would form part of his first trophy-winning side when the Reds clinched the FA Cup in 1948.

Even though the pre-war system had delivered such a wealth of talent to the club, Busby and the board wanted to improve things even further, especially as the number of genuine prospects coming through the system immediately after the war was disappointing. There were several benefits in developing United's youth recruitment efforts. Signing a player in his early to mid teens ensured the club did not have to pay a transfer fee, so there was an economic reason for having a good youth policy. This was particularly important in the post-war era when United were still paying off debts from building Old Trafford, and also faced the additional costs of rebuilding the ground, which had been bombed during the war. In those circumstances, a good youth policy was a financial necessity.

But that wasn't all. In his first years as manager, Busby had to deal with a couple of incidents where established players had caused him problems over financial issues. Morris, a creative and goal-scoring inside-forward, was sold to Derby County in March 1949 for a record fee of £24,500 after he had demanded extra money once too often (though the final straw was when he walked off the training pitch after a row with Busby). Then, when United toured the USA in the summer of 1950, Mitten was lured to play in Colombia for Santa Fé, when he was offered a £5,000 signing-on fee and a salary of £5,000 a year, plus bonuses (at the time, the maximum wage in England was just £12 per week, and would rise to £14 in June 1951).

Although both of these men had admittedly come through the United ranks, they were also war veterans and so were never going to be easily 'managed'. Busby believed that if he could bring up players 'the United way' – his way – such incidents would be much less likely to happen. He wanted to create world-class players, and 'to do the job efficiently [I] had to get hold of them young – as soon as they were available, in fact'. A devout Catholic, Busby had learned his lesson well from the Jesuits.

He was also quoted as saying: 'I do not believe you can buy success.' So an enhanced youth policy was the way forward, and when Rocca died on 13 June 1950, Busby had a ready-made replacement to head up the scouting network. Joe Armstrong was a friend of the manager's from his playing days at Manchester City, and he had started scouting for the club in 1947 (and possibly even earlier than that).

The man Busby referred to as a 'gentleman ferret', for the way he would unearth talent, had a simple set-up. In all, he had a team of no more than eight scouts working across the whole of England, with a further three in Ireland. They would feed in information to him about the best players they had seen, while Armstrong would also get letters sent in from teachers extolling the virtues of their young players. Those who seemed like good prospects were duly watched by the scouts.

This system was how Bobby Charlton came to join United. Ashington Stuart Hemingway headmaster, who had previously taught at Manchester Grammar School, sent in a letter recommending Charlton, and Armstrong himself went to watch the youngster in action for East Northumberland against Hebburn and Jarrow Boys on 9 February 1953. This was quite a low level of football, but Armstrong was impressed and got in quickly to sign up his player. Just as well, as soon Charlton was playing for England Schoolboys and the rest of the nation's scouting network was suddenly on to him.

But it wasn't just about spotting a player or getting to him first; it was also about persuading him to come to United. Armstrong worked in the GPO and from that job had learned to be a good communicator and well organised; he also had an excellent memory. But his main talent lay in the way he was able to persuade families that their son's best interests lay in joining United, where he would be well looked after. Armstrong's son Joe Junior recalls: 'He was persuasive, good in company and always charmed the mothers . . . the key figure to win over.'

This wasn't just a sales pitch; Busby ensured he had the best team of people looking after his often shy and nervous young recruits. Not only were the digs the club found for the players often more comfortable than the accommodation they would have known at home, but he employed excellent coaches such as Bert Whalley to work with his assistant Jimmy Murphy (who also managed the youth side). Whalley was not only a good influence, but also brought to his role a professional level of attention to detail, readying the players for the step up to senior level. Trainer Tom Curry completed the back-up team. From now on, recruiting the best talent would be a top priority, and United were going to scour not just the Manchester area but the whole of the British Isles in search of the very brightest prospects.

Soon the word went round the grapevine that United was the best place for ambitious young footballers to go. It helped, of course, that Busby was having success with the first team, but players liked coming to a major club (not something United had been able to claim between the wars), they knew the coaches would improve them as players, and United had a reputation as a family club (and Busby was keen to recruit players for whom family was an important element in their life). However, probably the biggest draw was that they saw they would get their chance as soon as they were ready, for Busby was always quick to give his kids a go in the first team if he thought they were good enough.

There was one other reason why Busby wanted to bring in so many young players: he had an innate trust in their ability to play with a freedom and excitement that would ensure Manchester United played football the right way. If he fielded such a side, he knew he would earn the enthusiastic support of the fans.

The FA Youth Challenge Cup was exactly what Busby wanted to test his youngsters against the best of the rest. Indeed, the competition could not have been set up at a better time as far as he was concerned: he knew he had a group of youngsters who were capable of taking on anyone, and now he had the way of proving it. He had realised that many of his post-war side would be coming to the end of their careers soon, and so had been working to ensure he had ready-made replacements coming through at this time. More to the point, he had one player in his team that he and Murphy reckoned to be the best prospect they had ever seen: Duncan Edwards.

Busby had first received reports on the young lad from Dudley as early as 1948, but it wasn't until the night of 2 June 1952 that Murphy and Whalley finally went to his house and got his signature, some four months before he turned 16. Although he was at the bottom end of the age range allowed to compete in the Youth Cup, Busby and Murphy had no hesitation in throwing him into action once they had seen just how good a player he was.

In the first round, his youngsters met Leeds United on 22 October and won 4–0, helped on their way by an own goal from Jack Charlton. Then United ran up an incredible 23–0 scoreline against Nantwich in the second round – still a record in the competition. They went on to beat Bury and Everton, attracting ever-increasing crowds as they did so, as the press began to build up the players – particularly Edwards – as the stars of the future. In the quarter-finals, the Reds went to Barnsley, where they were watched by a crowd bigger than the one that saw the Yorkshire club's first team in action later that day. United's youth team was that big a draw. They then won the two-legged semi-final 7–2 on aggregate against Brentford to set up an eagerly anticipated final.

In that final, Busby's side came up against Wolverhampton Wanderers, who were to be United's biggest rivals at senior level throughout the rest of the 1950s (Wolves would finish in the top three of the league every season bar one until 1961). The first leg took place at Old Trafford and 20,934 came to see a thrilling display by the home team, who crushed Wolves 7–1. The side that day featured Eddie Colman, Ronnie Cope, Duncan Edwards, David Pegg, Albert Scanlon and Liam Whelan, all of whom would go on to have significant careers at United. With the tie effectively over, United went to Molineux for the second leg and drew 2–2.

Having set such a high standard in the first year, United went on to win the Youth Cup for the next four seasons. In the process, they gave a chance to a whole range of up-and-coming stars, such as Shay Brennan, Bobby Charlton, Alex Dawson, David Gaskell, Wilf McGuinness and Mark Pearson, who would also make their mark on the club.

When United did finally lose their grip on the Youth Cup, during the 1957–58 season, there was a much more serious tragedy occupying everyone's minds. The Munich Air Disaster of 6 February 1958 ended the lives of eight of the 'Busby Babes' as they returned from qualifying for the semi-finals of the European Cup. By this stage, many of the products of the youth system were now in action for the senior side. The club's youthful first team played an exhilarating brand of football that had captivated the nation and reflected the spirit of the era, where rock'n'roll and teen culture were transforming a nation that had had enough of post-war austerity.

Gentlemen Ferrets and the Busby Legacy

In 1955–56, the club had won the league title, which earned them an invitation to play in the European Cup. The previous year (the competition's first), champions Chelsea had been forbidden to enter by Alan Hardaker of the Football League, who worried that the new continental distraction would damage his competition. Busby did not see it that way, and gained the backing of both club chairman Harold Hardman and Sir Stanley Rous at the FA to ensure United could take part. The latter saw it as an opportunity for an English club to pick up some continental experience, following the shock of England's Wembley defeat to Hungary in 1953 and another disappointing display in the 1954 World Cup, and disagreed with Hardaker about the likely drawbacks. Rous, like Busby, knew that English football had to move with the times.

Despite Hardaker's doubts, the European Cup proved an instant hit with the fans, and this was one further reason why the Busby Babes became arguably the first team to have a national following in England. At Munich, Colman, Edwards, Pegg and Whelan, four graduates of the Youth Cup sides, were among those who perished. That horrific disaster not only cemented the significance of the European Cup in the history of the club, it also ensured that the Youth Cup would always be treated with a special seriousness at United – something as true today as when it was first contested some 60 years ago.

Given the massive impact that Munich had on United, it was perhaps not surprising that it took a while before the club was able to restore its dominance of the Youth Cup. And when the Reds did next reach the final in 1964, there was another young lad who was getting all the attention in just the same way that Edwards had a decade before. His name was George Best.

United had a bye in the first round and then destroyed Barrow 14–1 before coming through the next two rounds with much closer wins over Blackpool (3–2) and Sheffield United (2–0). In the quarter-finals, old rivals Wolves lay in wait, but after another 3–2 victory the Reds were through to the semi-finals, where local foes Manchester City stood between them and a sixth Youth Cup final.

Given Busby's insistence that United's scouting system should at the very least attract the best of the local talent, not to mention that from across the nation, there was a lot riding on this game. Both teams featured plenty of players from Manchester and surrounding areas; and both had some seriously bright prospects in their ranks (already five from City and three from United had played for their first team when the two sides met for the first leg of the semi-final on Wednesday 8 April 1964).

Old Trafford hosted the first game, and a crowd of 29,706 turned up to see who would earn local bragging rights. Busby had always worked on the basis that preparation for the Youth Cup should be as similar as possible to the arrangements in place for the first team. For him and Murphy, this was just as important business as what the first team did – and woe betide anyone who believed it was just a matter of a bunch of talented kids having a kickabout. This was a first chance for the players to prove themselves; and those who fell short when the pressure was on were unlikely to be given a second chance. Unlike City, the entire United side had already signed professional forms.

Thus far, Best had not played in the tournament, but it was a mark of just how seriously the game was viewed by Busby that he was drafted in for this one, even though he had played for the first team on the Saturday and the Monday before. United's Bobby Noble was also left in no doubt that he was to give no quarter in ensuring he stopped his opponent, when Murphy said to him: 'Remember, son, they can't run anywhere without ankles.'

It proved to be just as passionate a game as any first-team derby, with hefty challenges of the sort that would never be allowed nowadays flying in from both sides. Albert Kinsey scored a hat-trick, with David Sadler adding the other, as United ran out 4–1 winners, but the press were more concerned about the aggression shown on the pitch and called for calm in the second leg 12 days later.

At Maine Road, in front of a crowd of 20,000, United ensured there would be no comeback when they took the lead on the night with an own goal after 18 minutes. After a City equaliser, early second-half goals from Sadler and Best gave United an even greater margin of comfort and the game eventually finished 4–3 (Sadler scored again) for an 8–4 aggregate win.

Having won the grudge match, United then faced Swindon Town in the final. This was expected to be an easier game than the semi-final, and so it proved, with Best unstoppable and Sadler scoring three goals as United completed a 5–2 aggregate win. John Aston Jr, Best, John Fitzpatrick and Sadler from the team all went on to have long careers at United; skipper Noble had his progress ended by a serious injury; and goalkeeper Jimmy Rimmer eventually left United in 1972, unable to depose Alex Stepney, and went on to appear for Aston Villa in the 1982 European Cup final, 14 years after Aston, Best and Sadler had done so for United.

Just as had happened in the 1950s, Youth Cup success was soon followed by first-team glory, as United won the league title in 1964–65 and 1966–67, before winning the European Cup in 1968 with a side that featured eight players who had come through the ranks at United. This pattern was something that was specific to United; when most other sides won the Youth Cup, it did not lead on to league success soon after. Even when this did happen, as when Everton and Arsenal won the trophy a few years before going on to take the league in 1970 and 1971 respectively, hardly any of the former Youth Cup side were involved in the senior triumph.

From the beginning, Busby had known how important the Youth Cup could be, and had instilled this belief in the club. United fans had come to recognise the link as well, and in a way that was arguably unique to the Reds. But when Busby first retired in 1969, ushering in a period when the club had a series of managers all trying to emerge from his shadow, the Youth Cup began to fall down the list of priorities. The new managers – Wilf McGuinness, Frank O'Farrell, Tommy Docherty and David Sexton – all had enough on their hands trying to get the first team back to the top where it had been under Busby. The 1970s became an era when there were fewer top-class youngsters coming through, with Arthur Albiston, Mike Duxbury, Brian Greenhoff and Jimmy Nicholl among the most significant juniors to emerge from United's youth scheme.

However, when Ron Atkinson took charge of United in the summer of 1981, he was able to benefit from a genuine prodigy in his ranks who had been spotted by one of his predecessor's scouts: Norman Whiteside. He also made a highly significant appointment on his arrival. Eric Harrison had become available after Everton had sacked manager Gordon Lee and new boss Howard Kendall wanted to bring in his own men. Atkinson, like Kendall, was in the process of revamping United's entire backroom staff, and he believed Harrison would be the man to revitalise and revolutionise the youth team.

Despite his reputation for being a bit flash, Atkinson worked hard, was extremely dedicated to his task, and – although he was more than happy to spend big in the transfer market – he knew that a good youth set-up would pay dividends. Even though he had not been the club's first choice in the role, he had the confidence to start planning for the long-term future, something that few of his predecessors had been able to do properly.

The results were quick in coming. Harrison's juniors reached the Youth Cup final in 1982. The line-up featured Clayton Blackmore, Graeme Hogg, Mark Hughes and Whiteside – one of the most impressive pools of young talent United had brought together since the 1960s. Sadly, it wasn't quite enough as they lost out 7–6 on aggregate to Watford.

Four years later, United were back in the final – this time against Manchester City – but again they fell short, losing 3–1 on aggregate, with a side that featured goalkeeper Gary Walsh and full-back Lee Martin, who was to play a significant role under United's next manager. But in truth, Walsh had been the Reds' star performer in the final, and without him the margin of defeat could have been much greater.

In some ways, these two final defeats reflected the rest of Atkinson's career at United: the club did much better, winning the FA Cup in 1983 and 1985, and never finished lower than fourth under his charge. But just as importantly, they also never finished any higher than third in the table. United had become a very good side, with strength throughout the club, but they weren't the best. In November 1986, the board decided to change all that: Atkinson was out, and in his place came a young Scottish manager who had done extraordinary things in his previous job at Aberdeen – Alex Ferguson.

While results were not instantly transformed on the pitch, off it everything changed as soon as Ferguson arrived at Old Trafford. He immediately told Harrison that he wanted more players to come through to the senior side from the youth ranks. The youth coach remembers being told that United were 'miles short of perfection' and 'great underachievers'. Ferguson's assistant Archie Knox commented that Aberdeen's youth side would easily beat United's. Harrison, who could be just as fiery as Ferguson and Knox, responded to these challenges by saying: 'Get me some better material to work with and I will produce more first-team players for you.'

Harrison was right. At the time, United were often losing out on the best young talent being produced in Manchester, which was increasingly finding its way to City. Part of the reason was that the club's scouting system was out of date. Prior to a teachers' strike in the early 1980s, most of the best talent came from the schools, and it was there that clubs had traditionally looked for their recruits. But after the strike, which resulted in teachers drastically cutting back on their after-school activities, it was the Sunday morning junior clubs that were producing the best young players. United had not caught up with events and needed to adapt.

As an immediate gesture, Ferguson and Knox recruited four local lads to the club. It wasn't so much about getting the best, but about sending out a message that United was the home for Manchester kids to come to play football.

Fortunately, both Ferguson and Harrison recognised that the other was hard-working and would settle only for the best, so any arguments that ensued were quickly forgotten in the mutual drive for greater success. Ferguson took on board Harrison's recommendation and gave the scouting system a huge boost, eventually increasing their number to about 40 paid staff, with Les Kershaw becoming chief scout. Ferguson also re-energised them, as Harrison recalls: 'He made them feel important, no, vital to his ambitions.' Thus inspired to work all hours in all conditions, the scouts set about finding as many of the best players as they could. They knew they weren't being asked to find the best kids in the street or the town, but the best in their region.

Kershaw was recruited from Arsenal by the manager soon after he arrived at the club. As chief scout, Kershaw's role involved not only planning which scouts would go to which games – and ensuring they had tickets for the matches – but also watching a lot of football himself. He would keep an eye on players with links to the club who were at the FA School of Excellence in Lilleshall, ensuring they did not feel forgotten while they were there, but he would also go to watch schoolboy football or even players at other clubs. Each week he reckoned he would have about a dozen scouts at league games, with a couple at non-league games. It wasn't long before he had a network in place that meant he could state: 'Any player good enough for United will have already been spotted by the age of fourteen.' Another element that Kershaw improved was the training of the club's scouts 'so that they know exactly how to assess and analyse a match in a clinical way'.

What was more, when the young lads turned up at United for their trials, Ferguson would almost always be there, watching on. His presence loomed over them all. For some lads, this may have been intimidating, but those who thrived under the spotlight were the ones United wanted in any case. It also showed them that the route to the first team was open, and that the manager cared. At so many other clubs, players have commented on how distant the manager seemed from them. That was not the case at United; even now, Ferguson gets to know all his players and their families.

Soon Harrison brought in another recruit for the club's youth set-up: Brian Kidd. The two had worked together at Everton some years before, and Kidd had just returned to the UK from the USA when a vacancy arose. Knowing his man, and knowing his background as a European Cup winner who had played alongside Best, Law and Charlton, Harrison believed Kidd would be both a supportive figure to the youngsters and an inspirational one, having seen life at the very top of the game. Kidd became United's youth development officer and also managed the 'B' side, initially on a part-time basis. One of Kidd's roles was to get out to the Sunday junior leagues, and his success in doing that was instrumental in United picking up the best players around. As United's youth development officer, he also spent a great deal of time going to schools to represent the club, before in 1991 he stepped up to become Ferguson's assistant.

The pieces of the jigsaw were in place; now it was just a matter of bringing it all together so that the scouting network delivered the players, the youth coaches trained them in the United way, and then the manager was ready to give them their chance. It sounds simple, and when it works it looks simple, too. Though it didn't happen at once, there were soon plenty of signs that the future was bright. Especially when, about a year after the arrival of Ferguson, he and scout Joe Brown set off to Swinton to give a dark-haired young lad the 14th birthday present of his dreams: a contract with United. For Harrison, this boy was to be the 'springboard' for all that followed. Whatever they had heard about him, and whatever they hoped he might go on to achieve, it is fair to say that Ryan Giggs surpassed all their expectations. But first he would help the Reds win their first Youth Cup in over a generation.

2

How to Impress a Mop and Other Lessons

'The most important thing wasn't being at United. It was working hard enough to make sure they'd let me stay there.'

David Beckham

Second Round: Wednesday 27 November 1991, Roker Park
Sunderland 2 Manchester United 4
Team: Pilkington; Gordon, Neville, O'Kane, Switzer; Gillespie, Butt (Beckham), Davies, Thornley; McKee, Savage.
Sub not used: Casper.
Goals: McKee (2), Savage, Gillespie

By the time United's 1991–92 FA Youth Cup campaign got under way in November (as one of the bigger clubs, United received a bye until the second round), most of the attention in the *Manchester Evening News* was focused on Ryan Giggs – and he wasn't even in the team to go to Wearside. The coverage was partly because the young Welsh prodigy had broken into the first team and was attracting attention beyond the confines of the local newspaper. Already a star, Giggs was always the biggest story going in the youth team that season. He was omitted from the trip to the Northeast because manager Alex Ferguson wanted to keep him fresh for the weekend, when the first team were due to visit Crystal Palace, as they continued their pursuit of a first league title in 25 years. He added: 'We've also kept him out in fairness to the youth strikers.'

But there was another, more specific, reason why Giggs was getting so much press coverage: that week he celebrated his 18th birthday. Mark Hughes commented: 'When I was his age, I was struggling to get into the "A" team, never mind hitting the headlines in the first team. That tells you about his remarkable progress and his ability. He is a great young player, one in a million.' Meanwhile, club captain Bryan Robson stated that the presence of Giggs, Lee Sharpe and the other young players at United had been a factor in persuading him to sign another contract to stay at the club. Clearly, there were many who felt the future was looking very bright for the Reds.

For the apprentices, getting into the Youth Cup side was seen as a vital stepping stone. And the club treated it that way, too. Not only did the pre-match routine replicate that of the seniors, but Harrison would always have future Youth Cup opponents watched beforehand, just as the first XI would do when they prepared for a match. This was not something done for league fixtures played by the club's apprentices. But even for regular games, Harrison would drum into his sides that they must always respect the opposition and the match officials.

There is little doubt that United, probably above all other clubs, emphasised the importance of this tournament to their youngsters. Because of the history attached to the Youth Cup at Old Trafford, it had a special place in the club's calendar. So there was a sense of eager anticipation among the apprentices when the line-up for the first game was chosen. The first-years knew this was the biggest game of their United careers to date, while for the second-years it was a chance to build on their previous achievements.

In goal was Kevin Pilkington, who had joined the club only a matter of months ago after he'd been spotted in action in Grantham by Midlands scout Ray Medwell. In front of him were full-backs Mark Gordon and local lad George Switzer, while the central defensive pairing was John O'Kane from Nottingham and Gary Neville. The midfield featured two speedsters on the wings: Keith Gillespie and Ben Thornley. In the centre were captain Simon Davies and Manchester boy Nicky Butt. Up front were Glaswegian Colin McKee, one of the most experienced players in the side, and Welshman Robbie Savage. Midfielder David Beckham and defender Chris Casper were on the bench. Paul Scholes missed out entirely.

For Davies, it was a proud moment when he was chosen to be captain. He recalls that the first game the apprentices played after he had been given the armband, he ran out from the tunnel on to the pitch at the front of the team. It was only when he'd reached the centre circle that he looked back, and saw the rest of the side still standing there, laughing hysterically at setting up their skipper. It was a sign of a group of lads who were confident, relaxed and eager to enjoy themselves.

The team went into the tie in confident mood. The previous year, United had done well in the Youth Cup. They began by beating Darlington 6–0 away, defeated Everton after a replay, overcame Liverpool 3–1 away, and finally saw off Southampton 2–0 away to reach the semi-finals. Barring their way to the finals were Sheffield Wednesday. A 1–1 draw in Sheffield saw United go into the second leg as favourites, but when they lost that game 1–0 the chance was gone for another season, and the wait to reclaim the Youth Cup continued. Among the players who were back for a second chance in 1991–92 were not only Giggs, but also Raphael Burke, Davies, Gordon, McKee and Switzer, who would all play their parts in the Youth Cup run.

By now, with the regular season three months old, the second-year apprentices had settled in to working with the first-years, and it was becoming clear to those inside the club that United had a youth side with good potential. But the news hadn't spread far. Under the heading 'Red Babes Top The Hit Parade', the match report in the *Manchester Evening News* for the second-round tie ran to just 79 words. At this stage, there was little sense from the paper that something special was in the offing, deserving in-depth coverage. Despite this, United were reported to be 'a class apart', with McKee and 'Robert' Savage, United's two strikers, both scoring in the first ten minutes, the latter with a header. By half time, McKee had added a third and Northern Irishman Gillespie scored a fourth to leave the side in cruise control. Sunderland's two goals weren't even deemed worthy of mention. McKee remembers feeling that the first game in a cup run is always a tough one, so for United to come through so easily gave them all a confidence boost.

It was all very low-key, but then that was how Ferguson and youth manager Eric Harrison liked it; they didn't want too much hype or attention given to the young prospects. Certainly, there was little chance for the apprentices at the club to get too cocky; as we will see, they were very much kept in their place by those more senior in the United hierarchy. Harrison's comment afterwards – 'They took me to the heights and depths, both on the same evening' – showed that he was not a man easily satisfied.

However, to get even this far, the apprentices had had to show a special talent that made them stand out from so many other hopefuls along the way. A few of them had been attached to United since they were about nine, but the first significant step came at 14 when the brightest prospects were offered schoolboy terms. For the next two years, they continued to train with the club in the evenings and play regular games for the junior sides, usually on Sunday mornings. During school holidays they would often come to United for training camps as well. Savage, who came from Wrexham, remembers this period as the time when he first had the chance to play alongside the first-year apprentices and got an early taste of life in digs. There were also tournaments in Switzerland during school holidays to be enjoyed.

After two years on schoolboy terms, the chosen few were given apprentice contracts. For the first-years in the Class of 92, they signed their apprentice forms and began to be officially employed by United on 8 July 1991. Within a couple of weeks, they were taking part in the Milk Cup tournament, held in Coleraine in Northern Ireland. It was an early chance for the newcomers to spend some time together and get to know each other away from the day-to-day work in Manchester. Beckham was named captain of the squad, perhaps partly because Nobby Stiles, who was in charge, knew him better than some of the others, as he'd coached him when the Londoner had made previous trips up to Manchester.

The trip gave them the opportunity to show off their new United tracksuits, but also provided them with a way to get to understand a bit more of the history of the club. The squad were staying at a hotel owned by Munich survivor Harry Gregg, a man who had played alongside many of the graduates of United's first great Youth Cup side. The club always worked hard to try to give their youngsters some idea of the legacy they were inheriting. Unsurprisingly, not all of them paid too much attention to this – they were entirely focused on making their own way.

On 26 July the new apprentices duly won their first piece of silverware as United employees. Thornley, who was named Player of the Tournament, and Savage scored the goals in their 2–0 win over Hearts. Butt, Gillespie, Neville and O'Kane also formed part of that winning side. It was the best possible start to their career and gave them early encouragement for the season that was to come.

Although the FA Youth Cup was the most prestigious part of the apprentices' career that season, there was also regular league action, usually in the 'B' and 'A' teams, as well as other knockout tournaments. The 'B' team played in the Lancashire League Division Two, while the 'A' team played in Division One. Just occasionally, the apprentices would get a chance at a higher level, playing in the Pontin's League for the Reserves. Unlike the other two leagues, here they would be playing alongside their senior colleagues – first-teamers returning from injury or battling to fight their way back into the side. Of all the Youth Cup squad, only McKee featured in the Pontin's League on a regular basis, making 20 appearances in total, and scoring 11 goals. O'Kane was the only one of the first-years to make even three starts in the league for the Reserves, perhaps because he was one of the more physically mature players.

After the success in Northern Ireland, the apprentices returned to Manchester to continue their preparation for the new campaign. The Lancashire League season got under way on 24 August, and United's 'A' team took on Tranmere Rovers at home – and promptly lost 5–0. The unlucky defence featured Neville, O'Kane and Switzer. At the other end, forwards McKee and Savage drew blanks, while mid-fielder Davies was unable to stem the tide in the centre. Casper and speedy winger Burke came on as substitutes, but could not change the pattern of the game. It was not the most auspicious of starts, though they put things right in their second fixture a week later, when they beat Bolton Wanderers 4–1 away from home, and Butt and Thornley got their first games for the 'A' team that season. After that erratic start, both 'A' and 'B' sides eventually finished second in their respective leagues, behind Crewe Alexandra in both cases. Looking back on it now, most of the players recall it as a period when they rarely, if ever, lost a game and as a time when the squad rapidly came together as a group.

With lads of this age, it was to be expected that they would be developing at different speeds and adapting to their new lives as professional footballers in different ways, so early upsets such as the one against Tranmere were not out of the ordinary. As ever, it was a case of how the players responded to a setback that said more about them than the fact that they had been beaten in the first place. The response was very encouraging.

With regular matches to enjoy, the first-year apprentices in 1991–92 also had the chance to earn some money for their work at United. In those days, the pay was just £29.50 a week (a rate set by the Youth Training Scheme, or YTS), with a further £10 each week towards transport costs. There were also win bonuses to be earned, usually £8 in the 'A' team. The apprentices also received two tickets for each of the first team's home games, and if they were playing away that day for one of the junior sides, they would often sell on their tickets to earn some extra cash. However, doing this carried its own risks, as Harrison would often ask the players specific questions about what had happened during the match. 'If they haven't [learned something], well they've not been watching close enough,' he said.

So, what was a typical day like for these 16-year-olds?

Work would begin at nine o'clock when the apprentices arrived at the Cliff, United's main training ground in those days in Broughton, to do their chores. Latecomers would be fined. The work might be polishing a senior player's boots, pumping up the training balls or cleaning the showers and changing rooms. 'Giving small jobs to them both here [at the Cliff] and at Old Trafford does give them a respect for their surroundings and helps keep their feet on the ground, too,' explained Harrison. Joe Roberts, who was one of those in charge of cleaning the first-teamers' boots, says it gave him the advantage of getting used to being around the seniors – something he believes would benefit the modern-day apprentices, who usually do not have to perform the same sort of tasks.

Then they would get ready in the apprentices' changing room (one of three at the Cliff; the Reserves and the first team each had their own room as well) and get on the bus to travel to the club's other training ground, at Littleton Road, close by in Lower Kersal, at ten. They would usually begin with a warm-up jog and a session of sprints before getting down to ball work and then team games.

One such game was line ball. While the goalkeepers went off to do separate work, the rest of the apprentices would split into two teams on a full-size pitch without goals. To score, you had to dribble the ball to the opposite goal-line and then put your foot on the ball. Each side would have one sweeper, but otherwise a player could tackle only his opposite number.

Ferguson and Harrison both agreed that, with lads of 16, it was important not to let them play too many games – Harrison reckoned that none would play more than 45 matches in a season. The reason for this was simple: at that age, he reasoned, 'few players have the tactical know-how. We have to teach them how to play the game and just throwing them into match after match won't do that.'

After training, they would do some gym work before showering and heading back to the Cliff for lunch. Afterwards, they would go to an area of the Cliff which they referred to as 'Little Wembley' to practise drills, such as free kicks and so on. Eventually, Harrison would say they could finish, and most were back home or in digs by four o'clock.

During these training sessions, the players were very aware that they had to impress Harrison, and they were all terrified of upsetting him. If he wasn't standing on the touchline, constantly urging them to do better, the players knew he would be watching them from his office inside the buildings at the Cliff. Their practice sessions and games were often accompanied by an unusual soundtrack, as Gillespie recalls: 'Everyone always talks about when we used to play at the Cliff and he used to watch the game from upstairs and if you did something wrong you just heard the window banging.' Butt adds: 'I don't know how it didn't go through.'

An error that wasn't greeted by the sound of glass nearly shattering was almost always worse. 'He'd be silent for ten seconds and you knew that he was coming down to the side of the pitch,' remembers Giggs. Soon, a furious Harrison would have joined them and be tearing strips off whoever it was that had done something wrong. Many of the Class of 92 have gone on record to say that being on the receiving end of a Harrison dressing-down was even worse than the Ferguson 'hairdryer' treatment.

Despite this, Harrison now says: 'They were the easiest group of players I've ever had to deal with, because of their

attitude and ambition. They knew they had to make sacrifices to succeed. But we gave them confidence and we pushed
them along.'

Furthermore, there was logic to Harrison's decision to
watch from his office inside the Cliff: he had a superb
overview from up there, so he could see things he might miss
standing on the touchline. But it also helped the players, too.
As Casper says: 'He let us get on with it, which is a great way
of coaching.' If he'd been right next to the action, the urge to
intervene frequently might have been much greater; as it was,
he had to make a special effort to do so.

However, this group of lads thrived on the pressure of constantly having to perform at their peak and making sure they
didn't let down their manager. As Beckham has recalled: 'The
most important thing wasn't being at United. It was working
hard enough to make sure they'd let me stay there.' Casper
echoes those sentiments when he says, 'You always knew
where you stood with [Harrison] ... You've got to be a strong
character to play for United, so if you couldn't take it from
him, then you'd struggle.'

While there is no doubt that Harrison played a crucial role
in setting standards high, he was helped by the fact that the
players soon tried to go one better. Neville remembers that
there was 'an unbelievable work ethic' among the first-year
apprentices. Some of the second-years poured scorn on him
for training so much, giving him the nickname 'Busy', but
soon most of the first-years were doing extra training
together, and he recalls how they began to overtake many of
the second-years in the pecking order.

For Neville, this extra effort was essential. He felt he was not as talented as many of those around him, so to compensate he knew he had to work harder than anyone else. In his earlier days, he'd been a midfielder, but he soon realised that he would never make it in that role. 'With the quality of midfield players we had, I just got moved backwards, fortunately for me,' he recalls. Like Beckham, he knew it was all about being able to stay on at United. If he could find the right role in the team, his chance to progress would be greater. His logic was undeniable.

It has often been said that Eric Cantona was the man who changed the training ethic at United, regularly staying behind to practise when most first-teamers in those days would head for home as soon as they could. Certainly, his example was an important one, but the Class of 92 were doing it before he arrived. No wonder that they would all be working together so successfully within a few years.

Things were slightly different for goalkeeper Pilkington, not least because he was still at school. He would stay in Manchester for long weekends from Friday mornings to Monday afternoons, so he could play with the team at the weekend and then work with goalkeeping coach Alan Hodgkinson on Mondays. He would do this specialist work first, before joining the rest of the squad for training on set pieces. This meant he was on the receiving end of rather fewer of Harrison's unique brand of motivational ploys than the others. However, he says of the youth-team manager: 'We all had the utmost respect for him; he was hard but fair.'

As well as their training, once a week the apprentices had to do some academic work. There were two options – as

Savage puts it in his memoirs, the brighter ones did a BTEC in business studies in Accrington (Gillespie, Neville and Casper joined him there), while the rest went to Manchester College. There would also be a day during the week when they would have to do chores around the club.

Current Youth Cup manager Paul McGuinness remembers how the Class of 92 would often come back to join in with the schoolboys after they had completed their academic studies. It was just a part of their commitment to the game – and their love of playing. For the boys, having a chance to play with the 'stars' of the Youth Cup side in the evenings was a bonus. Indeed, their commitment also extended to going to watch their forthcoming Youth Cup opponents in action. Once this group began to make the breakthrough into the senior side, they would still come into the gym to play with the schoolboys. McGuinness recalls one session where early on Beckham hit a long pass in a gym match, instead of the usual short balls everyone else was playing. Immediately, a 14-year-old Alex Bruce (son of Steve) was trying to do the same. The Class of 92 loved it all: their team-mates, the club and the game. That love inspired all who saw it in action.

However, at this stage, the first-year apprentices were still getting used to having more regular encounters with the senior players. While Robson might have commented to the press on how excited he was about the youngsters coming through, this didn't mean that he and the rest of the first-teamers were going to give them an easy ride to the top. The new apprentices very quickly learned their position in the club hierarchy: right at the bottom. Joe Roberts says affectionately that they were 'the light entertainment for the first team', but it was arguably more at the *Jackass* end of the light entertainment scale than *My Family*.

In those days, senior players instituted a range of initiation ceremonies that could prove highly embarrassing. Many of the Class of 92 have recalled one game they had to endure: they had to chat up a mop in front of everyone (often including many of the first team), coming up with sufficiently impressive lines to wow the cleaning implement. For the more shy characters among the apprentices, it was a truly mortifying experience. Neville, for example, who admits he 'dropped women completely' at this time, found it distinctly challenging. It was small consolation that they got to try out their corniest lines on a mop rather than an actual girl. Glaswegian McKee recalls: 'When you've done your turn, you can enjoy watching everyone else, but until then it was a bloody nightmare.'

If their chat-up lines were deemed to have worked, or even to have been appalling, the apprentices might then be obliged to go on to the next stage of the process: making love to Clayton Blackmore. Fortunately, it wasn't the real Blackmore they had to make love to, but a life-size cut-out of the tanned Welshman. For the equally well-tanned Welshman Savage, who even then was one of the more extrovert characters, this was a chance to give rein to his acting skills and give everyone a laugh, even if he admits he found it frightening.

On one occasion, Simon Davies actually refused to do this, and he was instead forced to hold a cup of water steady for as long as he could. He was so struck with nerves that his hand shook and he spilled most of the water; his team-mates immediately nicknamed him 'Shaky'. The apprentices' changing room was no place for the faint-hearted or the thin-skinned.

There were several punishments for doing these things wrong, or without sufficient enthusiasm. One was to be hit on the head with a ball wrapped up in a towel (this was known as getting the 'bongs'), another was to have the United logo rubbed on to your chest with a wire brush. Perhaps the worst penalty was being shut up in the club's giant tumble dryer and sent for a spin. According to Neville, one of the leading tormentors was Giggs, who was clearly revelling in his new-found status as a first-teamer.

These sorts of initiation rites may not have helped them become more skilful footballers but, as Neville adds, 'it helped to bond us'. Savage also didn't suffer any long-term ill effects and has commented: 'The lads who got through it became the best players the Premier League has ever seen.' Nowadays, such behaviour has largely been eradicated from football clubs, but 20 years ago this sort of thing – and far worse – was commonplace in almost every football club in the land. As for what went on in rugby clubs, it is probably best not to go there ...

Occasionally, even some of the senior players admitted things got a little out of hand, but mostly it remained within reasonable boundaries. The players knew that if it went too far, the coaching staff would step in. Indeed, club physiotherapist Jim McGregor wrote an annual pantomime for the first-year apprentices to perform: Savage ended up being cast as Snow White, while winger Thornley was his Prince Charming. The whole playing and coaching staff, including the manager, turned out to watch – it was an important part of integrating the newcomers into the club.

Another minor humiliation was known as 'Funny Movements', where the apprentices had to dance in as imaginative a way as possible to some music being played by a first-teamer. For Savage, this would eventually open up a whole new career that would take him all the way to *Strictly Come Dancing*.

Although all are agreed that there were no cliques among the new apprentices, there was a slight divide in that local lads such as Butt, Neville, Scholes, Switzer and Thornley were able to go home to their families, while those from further away – such as Beckham, Gillespie and Savage – went back to their digs.

One who fell slightly in between the two groups was defender Casper, who came from Burnley. He started off living in digs, but found it hard to settle. Like most of the lads, he had just left school 'and six weeks later you walk in to Manchester United at the Cliff. It's pretty daunting really, although you've been on trial and things like that, it's never the same. I started off in digs and I went home after about a week – I missed my mam's cooking, really.'

But while Casper might not have settled, Gillespie found the experience much more to his liking: 'Things were good. It was quite difficult at times because you finish in the afternoon and you come back to digs and it's just a case of sitting in your room watching TV. When I first moved, there were about seven or eight of us in digs, so we had our laughs. The landlady was brilliant, the food was fantastic – she really looked after us well.'

Given their meagre pay, there wasn't much chance to live extravagantly, so many of the apprentices would hang out in Salford Snooker Club. 'It was just a way of getting out of the digs, because it did get a bit boring at times,' says Gillespie. As Neville adds: 'We used to go in every afternoon and basically play snooker for money, really. Me and Cass [Casper] used to lose and get quite angry. They used to find us quite funny, I think, because we're both quite intense characters, and they were quite relaxed and they just used to take the mickey out of us, to be honest.'

Those who didn't want to play snooker might choose instead to keep Gillespie company in a bookie's shop close to the training ground at the Cliff. Savage, who shared digs with the young Irishman, as well as keeper Pilkington, recalls their room being littered with betting slips. He also admits that they weren't above taking advantage of their landlady on the odd occasion: 'I always remember that it was two houses built into one, so one side of the house was hers and one side was ours. When Brenda [Gosling] used to go out, we'd sneak into the kitchen and nick all the biscuits and things, because we weren't allowed into the kitchen unless Brenda was there.'

As ever with young lads, there was a lot of competition about who could look the smartest and who was the most stylish. One way of working on that was to spend time on a sunbed, which many of them did – though, perhaps unsurprisingly, Scholes was not one of them. But one person's cutting-edge style is another's fashion *faux pas*, and Savage was keen to be seen as the trend-setter. As Pilkington records: 'He'll kill me for saying this, but if there was a mirror there he'd look in it.'

The other pastime in those days was to go out shopping. This wasn't a case of stocking up on the latest and flashiest designer labels, however. Savage remembers a group of them going to Marks & Spencer in the Arndale Centre to buy some jogging pants that cost under a tenner – even Beckham, who even then had a reputation for always being one of the smartest and sharpest dressers. Roberts recalls how the Londoner would sometimes save up his entire wage for a fortnight or more so that he could splash out on a particularly smart shirt.

Despite their desire to look cool, most of the Class of 92 remember that Savage managed to find the money for some curious combinations. Thornley comments, 'He had an absolutely appalling dress sense.' Neville confirms it: 'He used to come in in purple tracksuit bottoms and pink Ralph Lauren shirts and shoes.' Butt remembers the colours slightly differently: 'Bright pinks and lemons and stuff like that', while Scholes was horrified by Savage's 'bright red trackie bottoms and a bright green shirt every day'. It probably won't come as much of a surprise to learn that Messrs Butt, Neville and Scholes did not approve of Savage's more colourful outfits, but even Giggs feels the same about his fellow Welshman: 'He's still got the same dress sense now.'

Partly because money was so tight, but also because, as Savage said, 'we were that scared of getting chucked out', there was remarkably little bad behaviour from the apprentices. Harrison reinforced that message: 'As far as I'm concerned, there's no drinking at all ... If I find out that they have stepped out of line in any way they'll be in trouble ... If they don't want to toe the line, well, they're no good to us.' For those reasons, the apprentices were very unlikely to be discovered partying late at night in the bars and clubs of Manchester, getting drunk or trying to pick up women. They were ambitious to progress and didn't want anything to get in the way of that happening.

Indeed, the discipline extended all the way to the players' digs. Club nutritionist Trevor Lea contacted all the landladies to explain what the apprentices should be eating. At the time the dietary focus was on pasta and energy-giving drinks. But the message wasn't always appreciated, as Harrison recalls: 'We found out that they were eating their dinner and then nipping down to the chip shop for a bag of chips.' However, as the senior players all bought in to the importance of a better diet, the apprentices soon learned what they had to give up if they wanted success. The reason was there in front of them every day, when they went to the Cliff to train, as the young lads would look on enviously at the cars driven by the older first-team players and see what lay in wait for them if they worked hard.

Of course, there were lots of pranks that went on. Left-back Switzer, who was a second-year apprentice, was the most notorious in this respect. 'He was a pain in the backside to be honest with you. He used to slaughter me,' says Neville, with a smile. Others recall how 'we'd be walking down the street and he'd shout out to a girl, and he'd hide behind a dustbin or a wall, and you'd turn round and the girl would be looking at you. He'd stitch you up.'

Perhaps surprisingly to some, Scholes was another joker who got up to similar pranks. As Butt remembers, when they were travelling together on the bus 'he was always the cheeky chappy'. If someone came upstairs 'he'd shout out something then hide behind a seat', leaving Butt to take the flak – a rare case of someone quite literally being the Butt of his humour!

Savage was on the receiving end from Switzer, too: 'He used to do all kinds of things, like cutting your underpants up.' Giggs remembers some more of his tricks: 'Cutting the end of your socks off, Vaseline in your boxer shorts – all those kinds of tricks; Deep Heat in your shorts – he did all that.'

Despite the pranks from their team-mates and the initiation ceremonies imposed by the senior players, no one was in any doubt that this was where they wanted to be. Gillespie was the one who had travelled furthest to be a part of the United set-up and was one of those that many of his team-mates believed had the best chance to make it, as he had such searing pace. He has this to say of what it felt like to arrive at Old Trafford: 'I was a Man United fan since I was a kid, so it's an old cliché but it was a dream come true. I had pictures plastered all over my bedroom walls, and there I am training next to them.'

Keith Robert Gillespie was born in Larne, a small port in County Antrim to the north of Belfast, on 18 February 1975. He was educated in the seaside town of Whitehead, a few miles to the south, at the primary school there, before moving on to Bangor Grammar School in County Down, across the Belfast Lough. This was perhaps a surprising move as the school had more of a reputation for rugby and hockey than football. But fortunately he was able to get his football fix elsewhere.

His father Harry explains how he joined United: 'He

played for St Andrews in the South Belfast League, and Joe Kincaid, who is a manager in the South Belfast League, brought Eddie Coulter, the United scout, along to the match one day.' Coulter remembered the occasion: 'The first thing that really came to my mind was that he had so much pace. He could catch pigeons, the boy. Very quick, smart – the rest of it is really history.'

Kincaid had set up the club, situated at Mountainview, just off the Shankill Road in Belfast, after returning from the 1986 World Cup in Mexico. Initially, he was asked to help out the Under-13s, but quickly realised that there was real potential in the area, as there were few opportunities available for young lads to develop their talents. Very shortly after taking up the role, Kincaid saw the 11-year-old Gillespie at a soccer school at Orangefield, and was immediately struck by his talent. As he subsequently told the *Belfast Telegraph*: 'He ran like Seb Coe and his skills were excellent. I knew straight away that he was going to be a great player. I approached his father Harry, explained a little about St Andrews and asked him if he'd like to bring Keith along to the club.'

Happily, Gillespie senior knew that this was the perfect opportunity for his football-mad son. In the club's first season, Gillespie helped St Andrews to win a trophy, and Kincaid was soon setting up sides for all age groups from Under-11s to Under-16s and very quickly began attracting scouts from many clubs in England and Scotland. As we will see with some of the other members of the Class of 92, who began their careers at Boundary Park in Oldham, playing alongside other talented footballers in a well-structured environment at an early age can pay huge dividends.

Kincaid, who ran the youngest side at the club, was absolutely clear about the sort of talent and personality he wanted at St Andrews; those who fell short of his tough standards did not get to join or were quickly asked to move elsewhere. It was an early introduction to the harsh realities of footballing excellence: if you don't work hard enough and you're not good enough, you will soon get left behind. But Gillespie blossomed.

Quickly, St Andrews became known as the best junior football club in the country, and the scale of Kincaid's achievement can be seen in the fact that on 15 November 2005 Northern Ireland took on Portugal with a team featuring seven graduates of the club, including Gillespie and Warren Feeney, who scored Northern Ireland's goal in a 1–1 draw. Also that season, six of Kincaid's protégés took on England, captained by another of the Class of 92, David Beckham, and beat them at Windsor Park.

But despite all of Kincaid's work and the talent-spotting skills of Coulter, who was responsible for bringing many other players – including current Reds star Jonny Evans – to United, Gillespie was still very raw when he came across the Irish Sea to Manchester. In fact, he made his first trip over in 1986, aged 11, but he signed in secret on 10 September 1988, when he and his family were brought over to watch United beat Middlesbrough 1–0, though the deal did not become official until his 14th birthday later in the season. Gillespie remembers how, the night before the match, Ferguson and his wife came to the hotel where he and his parents were staying and they had dinner together. 'When you're thirteen, that's quite a big thing,' he comments. As we will see throughout this book, Ferguson's efforts to make families feel welcome and his attention to detail over these matters were remarkable and often made a lasting impression.

Gillespie felt a great responsibility to perform at United, despite the daunting nature of the challenge, being so far from home. Just to make things that much tougher, the skinny dark-haired winger from Northern Ireland was already having to face up to comparisons with another player who answered to the same description and had made the same journey to the Old Trafford club: George Best. What was more, Best had also had a starring role in United's previous Youth Cup success back in 1964. Being touted as yet another 'new George Best' raised expectation levels very high indeed.

So, no pressure, then. In a television interview he gave at the time he was getting ready to come to England, he denied there was any pressure on him and simply stated that he was 'excited. Very excited.' But in truth, as he later recalled: 'It was nerve-racking. It was fortunate another Irish lad came across with me, Colin Murdock. It made things a little bit easier, but it was very nerve-racking because people have high hopes for you back home and you really didn't want to fail.'

Harrison saw that he had something to work with: 'Absolute flying machine, Keith, he really was. He was as quick as I've ever seen for a boy over five, ten yards – he was absolutely explosive. It was a problem for him certainly fitness-wise [when he came over] – he just wondered what had hit him when he first came over for his first pre-season. You know, he was miles behind the rest of the lads. I think settling in he was OK.' That pace was certainly what made him stand out for Davies: 'He could win a game on his own,' he says.

51

Former United player Jim Ryan, who had just rejoined the club at that stage and was in charge of the Reserves, remembers seeing Harrison drilling the apprentices, getting them to run laps to build up their fitness. He also noted that Gillespie was lagging behind, along with one other youngster, a little ginger-haired lad. He recalls: 'Scholesy was always lagging at the back with Keith Gillespie. I didn't know at the time that he had an asthmatic condition, but he was always eighty yards behind the rest of the group with Keith, who would turn out to be a really good runner but at the time he had no level of fitness. I was able to train on Saturday morning, then get back quickly and watch the "A" and "B" teams play at the Cliff. So when I saw Scholesy playing games, you could instantly tell that he was a player with that special kind of football brain.'

Fitness issues aside, Paul Aaron Scholes had little difficulty in settling in at United as he was very much a local lad. Born in Salford on 16 November 1974, he grew up on Middleton's Langley council estate, which had been built in the 1950s, halfway between Manchester and Rochdale, to house the overflowing population of Manchester. His father Stewart was a very decent footballer, who played club football locally. Nowadays, Langley is occasionally the subject of studies on the problems facing such estates, with echoes of the world of *Shameless*; but even then it was very far from being a smart place. As a boy, Paul would regularly hang out in the estate's park, hoping to get a game of football with some of the local lads, who were nearly always bigger and older than him. It was a tough environment in which to learn the game, but it taught him never to be intimidated by bigger lads.

After primary school at St Mary's on Wood Street in Langley, he then went to Cardinal Langley RC High School in Rochdale Road. His time there proved significant, as he was taught by Mike Coffey, a United scout. It was while playing in a local schools final at the age of 14 that United's youth development officer Brian Kidd, who was there to present the prizes, decided he should go for trials with the club. According to Scholes, an Oldham Athletic fan, he didn't need asking twice. As he recalls: 'I was at Oldham for a couple of years, when I was about eleven, twelve, but [United] were the biggest club and as soon as they came in for you that's where you wanted to be. Brian Kidd showed me round the ground. I was a little bit overawed, but you knew it was a great club and you wanted to be there.' However, Coffey remembers it slightly differently, saying: 'He was very reluctant and took a couple of days to be convinced.'

Kidd recalls that he had first seen Scholes in action even earlier than that – when he was working for the FA and ran a course at Middleton sports centre in the late 1980s. At that stage 'Scholesy was no size, but the ability he had was unbelievable'. He and a couple of his friends then went to work at the Centre of Excellence. Not long after, Kidd joined United and was surprised to see that Scholes was not on the club's books. He discovered that the youngster had gone to play at Oldham Athletic, who had a good youth set-up as well. United went via the proper channels to see if Scholes would consider signing for United, and Kidd spoke to Scholes's parents to see if they'd consider him coming to United. As he says: 'We wanted them to come to Manchester United for the right reasons.' And fortunately that is what eventually happened.

Whatever the precise route was to bring him to Old Trafford, by this stage Scholes had developed associations with various clubs, starting with Langley Furrow and St Thomas More's. However, the most important team for his development was Boundary Park in Oldham, where he joined up with Neville and Butt soon after he left primary school. Their link with the team he supported was a strong one, and taking the step to go to United would have been daunting, as Scholes himself admits. We will hear more about the influence this team would have on the Class of 92 later.

When Scholes first came to the Cliff, Kidd warned Harrison: 'He's only tiny; he's got ginger hair – you'll probably have a bit of a laugh. But he can't half play.' They soon noticed his quick feet and his innate footballing intelligence. He could also score any type of goal, from a tap-in to a header or a long-range shot. After that, it was just a case of waiting for him to develop physically and helping out in any way they could.

However, once Scholes signed apprentice forms in July 1991, things did not go particularly well for him during his first year. Harrison recalls: 'He had a hard time to start with, because he had a bit of bronchitis, knee problems [Osgood-Schlatter disease], and Paul was dead worried at one stage.' Indeed, there were other shortcomings, as Harrison pointed out: 'He has no real pace, no strength.' Scholes himself also felt under pressure to deliver and remembers that season as a frustrating one: 'I was the smallest one and I didn't play in the first year in 1992. There is a time when you wonder if you're going to make it and if you're ever going to grow, and thankfully I filled out a bit.'

It was to be one of the most surprising facts about the Class of 92 that one of their most distinguished and successful graduates did not play a single minute in the Youth Cup run. The club was happy to be patient with him, as his talent and commitment were clear to all. Giggs remembers: 'You never got fooled by his size, because he was tough and he could look after himself.' By his second year as an apprentice, with his injury problems behind him, and his physical development having progressed, he was rapidly emerging as one of the brightest talents among the apprentices. As Thornley states: 'From his first year to his second year, there was so much difference in his style of play and in the second year he just virtually ran the show.' Harrison certainly gave him the opportunity to do that: 'Like Ryan Giggs, we told Paul to go out and perform, while also thinking of the team.'

But while Scholes may have missed out on the Youth Cup run, he still made 11 league appearances for the 'A' team, scoring five goals, and 20 appearances for the 'B' team, scoring 13 times. If this was what he could do when not fully fit and still developing, the club were surely right to think that he could be something very special in the future.

Having won their first game in the Youth Cup, the apprentices did not have to look too far into the future themselves for their next opponents. This time, they would have a home tie to enjoy, which meant a chance to run out at Old Trafford – a ground they all wanted to become much more familiar with. If that was going to happen, they all realised who they were going to have to impress.

3

The Sound of Glass Almost Breaking

'Was I a father figure to them? No, I was the boss.'

Eric Harrison

Third Round: Tuesday 17 December 1991, Old Trafford
Manchester United 2 Walsall 1
Team: Pilkington; Gordon, Neville, O'Kane, Switzer; Gillespie, Butt, Davies, Thornley; McKee, Savage (Giggs).
Sub not used: Casper.
Goals: Thornley (17), Savage (27)

Having comprehensively beaten the youth team of Second Division Sunderland at Roker Park in the previous round, the visit of Fourth Division Walsall to Old Trafford should have held few terrors for United's Youth Cup side, especially when the team was given a late boost with the news that Ryan

Giggs would be available. 'He is keen to play with the boys he is growing up with, but youth coach Eric Harrison wants to keep faith with the team who have been playing while Ryan has been in the first team,' manager Alex Ferguson told the *Manchester Evening News*. 'So we will get him involved and keep him in reserve if things are not going our way.'

This policy of keeping the young Welshman in reserve made sense. Giggs had been in action at Stamford Bridge with the first team just two days earlier, and Ferguson was always conscious of not overplaying him, as he had missed only two of United's 19 league games thus far that season. He replaced David Beckham as one of the Reds' substitutes (just two were named in those days) in what was the only change to the line-up from the second round.

The game kicked off at seven o'clock at a waterlogged Old Trafford and, as had been the case in the previous round, United got off to the best possible start. After 17 minutes, Ben Thornley hit home from 15 yards out, then ten minutes later Robbie Savage doubled the lead (though the *Evening News* gave the credit to Nicky Butt).

From there, the Reds would have hoped to go on to win the game comfortably, but that was not how it developed. The Saddlers, with one of the best youth teams they'd had for many years, began to come back into the game and it needed a crucial block from full-back Mark Gordon to prevent the two sides going in at the break with a one-goal margin. After the interval, Simon Davies took charge of matters, going on a brilliant run before beating the keeper, only to see his shot cleared off the line by a defender. Seventeen minutes into the second half, when goalkeeper

Kevin Pilkington failed to gather the ball cleanly, Steve Winter reduced the arrears.

Playing with confidence now, the Walsall side pressed for a goal that would bring a replay, and this gave United the chance to counterattack. Thornley almost took advantage to make the game safe, but his shot hit the post. With the pressure mounting, Harrison decided it was time to bring on his super-sub, and Giggs replaced Savage with ten minutes to go. It still wasn't enough to turn the tide, and United were relieved to hear the final whistle. David Meek's report in the *Evening News* was headed 'Reds Struggle Through', and that summed up the general feeling that there was definitely room for improvement. As in the previous round, early dominance had not been maintained for the whole 90 minutes.

That sort of slacking from the very highest standards was something that one man was never going to forgive. As he comments now: 'It can be bad for your health; we'd start off well and then they'd come back at us.' Manager Eric Harrison expected total commitment all the time from his charges and, as we have seen in the previous chapter, his players knew what to expect if they fell short in any way.

When people talk about the Class of 92, they usually focus on Beckham, Giggs, Neville, Scholes and the rest, yet there is little doubt that Harrison is just as central a character in the story of United's Youth Cup run that year. To reinforce that point, in his memoirs Beckham credited him, along with his father and Alex Ferguson, as being among the three most significant figures in helping him to achieve what he has done. He is not alone in singling out the role that Harrison played in moulding the Class of 92 into the great players so many of them became. Almost everyone I spoke to while writing this book mentioned what a key role he had played in developing not only their careers but also their way of behaving in life in general.

The affection and respect with which he is spoken of by his former charges is striking; some have said of him that he was a father figure to the Class of 92. Certainly that is how John O'Kane describes him: 'He was like a dad. I didn't grow up with a dad, so he was the next thing. He looked after you.' Perhaps Harrison might have recognised this need with the Nottingham-born defender, as he was very understanding of what each of his players required from him, but usually he would say this was to misinterpret his role: 'Was I a father figure to them? No, I was the boss.' There was certainly never any doubt as to who was in charge of the youth team.

So how had he come to take on that role? Like many of the most successful coaches, Harrison had not been a particularly brilliant player. Born on 5 February 1938, he grew up in Hebden Bridge, a town on the borders of Lancashire and Yorkshire. He was educated at Burnley Road School in nearby Mytholmroyd before going on to Calder High School. He was keen on football from an early age, and would spend many hours practising his skills. However, he points out that this alone is never enough: 'Practice will always make you better, but a youngster needs advice too.'

This was a lesson that would guide his approach throughout his life – no matter who he was talking to, he would be willing to give them the best advice he could. Beckham has written of him: 'He'll tell me what he thinks, not what he thinks I want to hear.' Raphael Burke echoes that assessment, commenting that Harrison was always honest with his players – even if at the time it seemed as if he might be getting on their back. But he believes teenagers need that, as they often believe they know it all already: 'He wasn't there to be your friend. Discipline is needed and you have to be critical.' As Burke recognises, Harrison was under pressure to deliver for Manchester United and he had to do what was best for the club, which meant never allowing any slackness.

After leaving school, Harrison took his first steps in a career in professional football when he signed for Halifax Town, one of the clubs he supported as a child, as they were based just a few miles away from where he grew up. Although he made his first-team debut in 1957 while still a teenager, he was already thinking about the coaching methods of the manager. He noted how, during the week, players were encouraged to express themselves, but when it came to match day 'the manager's instructions completely ruined the week's training' as he preached a safety-first, cautious approach that left the team scared to take any risks in case they made a mistake.

A fierce and (as he admits) occasionally bad-tempered competitor on the pitch, Harrison played at wing-half, but was also keen to learn as much about the game as possible. He began to work on his coaching badges as soon as he could, and was a qualified coach by the time he was 21. Astonishingly, only one other person in the club had any coaching qualifications at the time. As someone who loved the game, he recognised this was a route that would provide him with a lifetime's involvement in the sport, while his time as a player might last no more than a dozen years. Because he worked on his technical understanding from such an early stage in his career, he quickly developed a natural instinct for spotting talent, even in the warm-up: 'I look for balance, poise and the way they kick the ball.'

In 1964, after he was refused a loyalty bonus, Harrison left his local club and signed for Hartlepools United (as they were then known) on the northeast coast. The club was in a bit of chaos at the time, and was going through a period of transition when managers rarely lasted even a season; former United star Allenby Chilton was one of those who got caught up in the revolving managerial door. But at the start of the 1965–66 season, the Pool found themselves with a young boss who was to be the first major formative influence on Harrison's coaching philosophy: Brian Clough.

As Harrison explains, Clough's methods were simple: 'He told every player in the team their role ... You did it or you were out of the team.' Even then, Clough was a disciplinarian, fining Harrison half his wages when he argued with the referee, after the manager had warned him against doing so beforehand. It taught him a lesson, especially as in those days a fine really did hit players hard in the pocket, and the loss of earnings did not go down well with his wife at home.

But strict discipline wasn't the only thing that Harrison picked up from Clough and then applied to the Class of 92. He also learned about the crucial importance of good organisation, especially in defence, and how vital it was that players understood their responsibilities within the team. This was not just about marking your man at set pieces, but also fulfilling your role properly. So, according to Clough, if you were in the side as a centre-forward to score goals, that's what you should do: score goals. Whereas some might tell a misfiring striker not to worry if he misses a chance, Clough would remind the player that he could always sign up someone else to score goals instead.

Clough explained his thinking to Harrison as follows: 'Football is a simple game, and if I can get everyone to play in their position properly, then I'll have a good team.' In practice, players had to be the best they could be and do their jobs properly or else they would be replaced. For Harrison, this meant he believed in 'putting demands' on his squad all the time. However, as we saw in the previous chapter, the Class of 92 were always willing to work very hard to maximise their talents in any case. They put demands on themselves that were almost as tough as any their manager could come up with.

Although Harrison played for Clough for just one season before moving on to Barrow, that period had a big impact on his approach and the two men developed a strong mutual respect. Indeed, Clough subsequently tried to bring him to work as a coach at Derby County, but Harrison wanted to continue with his playing career at the time and so turned him down.

After seeing out the rest of his career in various smaller clubs until 1972, Harrison was finally ready to make the move into coaching, and his first role came when Harry Catterick appointed him youth-team coach of Everton, with a warning that he had some challenging lads to control. They quickly learned that the new man was not someone they should try to take advantage of.

Harrison stayed at the Toffees until 1981, rising through the ranks until he reached the position of first-team coach. But it was in his early days at the club that he encountered the second major influence on his philosophy: Bill Shankly.

The former Liverpool manager had retired from the Anfield club in 1974 and found himself marginalised there, as the new team in charge didn't want to have such a legendary figure looming over them. With no outlet for his passion for the game, Shankly instead came to watch Everton training, as his house overlooked their Bellefield facility. Whenever Shankly visited, Harrison would take the opportunity to learn whatever he could from the inspirational Scot; in particular, he found out how Shankly motivated people.

Some of his ideas were simple, but they proved hugely effective. One training exercise Shankly recommended was to paint a line 25 metres long and get the players to pass the ball along that line – this was important because it encouraged them to get the basics right. Clearly, if they could not do the basics in those circumstances, how were they ever going to be able to pass the ball accurately under the pressure of a match situation? But equally, the more confident they were about their basic skills, the more comfortable they would be to use them in a tight match situation. Harrison adopted the idea with some modifications and would use it when he came to United later on. He recalls how Gary Neville was one of those who would spend hours working on this technique.

Harrison might have continued his career with the Merseyside club, but when Gordon Lee (who had taken charge in 1977) lost his job in 1981, he feared that he would also be on the way out when the new man, Howard Kendall, arrived. He left Everton in somewhat acrimonious circumstances. Fortunately, he wasn't out of a job for long, as another club also had a new manager and he had begun to make similarly sweeping changes to his backroom staff.

Ron Atkinson was appointed Manchester United manager in the summer of 1981 and he brought in Harrison to run the club's youth set-up. Given a free rein to develop junior football at United, Harrison set about creating footballers who knew how to play the game properly – the free-flowing passing game that the manager wanted from the first team, but which was also part of United's traditional footballing style. Both men understood the vital importance of having a consistent approach to the game from top to bottom of the club. There was no point in coaching them to play one way at junior level and then changing it when they reached the top.

Although the two men had very different personalities, with Atkinson outwardly quite flash and Harrison anything but, both shared an appetite for hard work and held similar footballing philosophies. True, Harrison was more of a disciplinarian – he once took one of his youth sides who had been beaten 5–0 at Bolton Wanderers on to the bus without showering and straight back to the Cliff for extra training – but they respected each other. As we saw in Chapter One, the results were quick to come through, and United reached the final of the Youth Cup in 1982 and 1986, losing on both occasions.

While United had made big strides forward with their youth set-up during Atkinson's reign, when he lost his job and Alex Ferguson took charge of the club in November

1986, the demand was to do even better at junior level. It was a challenge Harrison was ready to accept. Indeed, he now admits that coming to Old Trafford brought with it an enormous pressure: the legacy of the Busby Babes loomed over all that he did. United had a track record of bringing through young players that no other club could match. In his own mind, if he wanted to be counted a success, he had to provide United with a group of players that would stand comparison with the lads from the 1950s. That was why the apprentices heard him banging at the window of his office at the Cliff so often.

He continued to emphasise the importance of ball work as the key to developing players; it was, he believed, the best way to enhance their confidence on match day. Indeed, part of Harrison's philosophy with the youngsters was teaching them that doing the right thing was more important at that stage of their careers than winning. In an interview in 1994, he said: 'We attempt to impress upon them that winning isn't everything. The main object of playing football at a young age is to develop into a skilful footballer; youngsters get so uptight as it is when they play football matches, so often they don't need the added pressure of trying to win.'

The other element of his job was, he felt, to ensure that by the time players left him they were capable of having a career out of football. For a few, Harrison knew they would get their chance at United, but normally only one or two from each year could be expected to make the transition to the first team – if that. He stressed: 'If they don't make it at Old Trafford, it doesn't mean that they are a failure – they may still have fifteen years as a professional footballer [elsewhere].'

The Sound of Glass Almost Breaking

The careers of Keith Gillespie, Pilkington and Savage all show how successful he was in achieving that aim, which is just as much credit to his working methods as the successes of those who had (and still have) long careers at United. Davies, now coaching at youth level himself, recognises just how effective he was at this: 'However their careers panned out, he mapped the way they should be as people, the way they should conduct themselves around a football club.'

As well as his own motivational skills, Harrison also recognised that he had one specific advantage at United, when it came to schooling his youngsters, that few other clubs could come close to matching: he could use United's history to motivate his young charges to achieve their potential. They only had to look at the club honours board, and to think of the famous names that had gone before them, to know how close they were to achieving something they had dreamed of for years: becoming a hero of the Stretford End. To reinforce that link with the past, he brought in two people who had not only been home-grown stars at United, just as his players were hoping to become, but who had in fact gone on to win the most prestigious prizes of the lot.

Brian Kidd was a crucial part of his team. Born in Collyhurst, Manchester, on 29 May 1949, Kidd made his debut for United as an 18-year-old in the 1967 Charity Shield, and ended that season scoring a goal on his birthday for the club as they won the European Cup at Wembley, beating Benfica 4–1. A man who had played for Matt Busby alongside the likes of George Best, Bobby Charlton and Denis Law, Kidd was a part of the last great United side and his links with that golden age helped to inspire his young players.

Kidd had left the club in 1974, and subsequently played for Arsenal, Manchester City, Everton (during Harrison's time there) and Bolton before ending his career playing in the United States. When he returned to England in 1988, Harrison and Ferguson brought him in to help out with the youth system. Kidd not only personified United's history, but he was a great enthusiast for the game and the sort of warm character who could provide support and encouragement to the youngsters. What was more, being a local lad himself, Kidd quickly developed a strong network of contacts in the area to ensure United had the pick of the talent in the Greater Manchester region. Too often in the past, United had lost out to Manchester City in this respect.

Kidd worked in various roles for United's youth set-up: he was Harrison's assistant in the Youth Cup team, he managed the 'B' team, and then he was promoted to youth development officer, which gave him a much broader role at the club. Many of the players saw in Kidd an ally, as he was able to leave the 'bad cop' role to Harrison. Colin McKee says he was 'more of a joker' than some of the others. Giggs remembers how Kidd even gave him some of his old boots when he first became an apprentice, as in those days he barely had the money to buy a pair for himself. This role, as a buffer between the players and the managers (whether Harrison at junior level or Ferguson later on), was a crucial one.

Fortunately, Harrison was able to find a ready-made replacement for Kidd to look after the 'B' team – a man who could not only match Kidd's Collyhurst background, European Cup-winning feats and England international status, but trump them with two league titles and a World Cup winner's medal. Footballing CVs don't come much more impressive than that of Nobby Stiles.

Stiles was another Mancunian, born on 18 May 1942, who came through United's junior ranks to make his debut in 1960. Although famed for his dodgy eyesight and toothless grin, as a player he was instrumental in both England's and United's greatest successes in the 1960s. He could play either as a defensive midfielder or at centre-back, despite the fact that he was not a big man. But size did not matter to him; what he lacked in inches he more than made up for in his fierce competitive instincts. Famously, his combative nature during the 1966 World Cup led to members of the FA trying to pressurise Alf Ramsey into dropping him after he had committed a bad foul on Frenchman Jacques Simon. The manager asked if he had deliberately hurt his opponent, but Stiles replied: 'I swear I didn't mean it. My timing was bloody awful.' Ramsey took him at his word and threatened to resign if the FA didn't back down, so Stiles went on to play a vital role on England's greatest footballing day.

Busby was just as clear about how important Stiles was to his side. Along with Paddy Crerand, he was the man who gave licence to the club's famed attacking talents to do the damage at the other end. And while he may not have had quite the same skills as Best, Law and Charlton, he was a very tidy footballer who could pick a pass just as well as he could break up an opposition attack.

After more than a decade in United's first team, Stiles left Old Trafford in the summer of 1971 and had brief careers at Middlesbrough and Preston North End (playing for Bobby Charlton) before moving into management. He started at

Preston and then went to Canada before returning to the UK for a brief spell at West Bromwich Albion.

With this background, Stiles had nothing left to prove to anyone, and only his infectious enthusiasm, great sense of humour and a massive amount of experience to pass on to the schoolboys and apprentices who made up the 'B' team. But, as one would expect from Stiles, his message was not simply about enjoying the game; according to Neville, he explained how 'you had to win the fight' as well. He once sent out the team with the message: 'Your best friends out there are your six studs.' It was a line he would have heard many times before from Jimmy Murphy, Busby's assistant and manager of United's Youth Cup sides in the 1950s, who also made sure his players understood that football is a physical game just as much as a skilful one.

Harrison, Kidd and Stiles – it was a formidable combination, and one that the lads who made up the Class of 92 were thrilled to work with. Beckham remembers when he first started coming to Manchester after signing as a schoolboy that Stiles was his regular coach and he made a strong early impression on him – and not just because his father told him what a great player he had been. 'Nobby was really hard . . . but I think he cared more about the youngsters he worked with than anything else in the world.'

If the players felt this, it was clearly a great benefit, but even more than that, Stiles made sure their parents understood his commitment to their sons. The Class of 92 were in very good hands. They knew it too – McKee says: 'You've got a World Cup-winning guy coaching you at fifteen – it doesn't get any better than that, does it?'

The Sound of Glass Almost Breaking

It was therefore something of a disappointment to many of them when, in August 1991, Kidd was promoted to become Ferguson's assistant, after Archie Knox had left the club at the end of the previous campaign. However, Kidd continued to keep a close eye on his former charges, and when the time came for them to be considered for senior action, many of the players felt reassured that they were going to be reunited with their old mentor.

Of course, it wasn't just those who were charged with looking after the youth set-up who made the Class of 92 feel special. As we have seen, the manager always seemed to be watching what they did and made sure he knew the players (and their families). Furthermore, Ferguson would often go to their games accompanied by Bobby Charlton, the man who more than any other personified what was expected of someone if they wanted to become a true United legend. In short, if you weren't inspired to do your best by all this, then you really weren't going to be inspired by anything. Charlton's involvement showed the families of the kids that they were already a part of something special at United, and that they had to treat the opportunity with great respect.

For all the club's efforts to show the youth team how important they were to it, the message didn't always sink in as much as might have been expected. Interestingly, Joe Roberts has this to say about the way the club surrounded its youngsters with former United heroes: 'At the time I didn't really think about it. Brian Kidd and Nobby Stiles were just there, helping us. But now I realise just what a great opportunity it was to work with people who had won the European Cup and the World Cup. I was so lucky to have that experience.'

Harrison has admitted in his memoirs that he could sometimes be too outspoken during his period as first-team coach at Everton: where previously he had been able to get away with a blunt assessment of a teenager's error, the same approach with a seasoned international could often have a counterproductive result. From his experiences on Merseyside, he learned the importance of tailoring his feedback to his audience. This didn't mean that he wouldn't dish out harsh criticism when he felt it was warranted, but he also understood the equal if not greater importance of encouragement and praise, and how to ensure that when he gave it out it had the maximum impact.

When dealing with shy 16-year-olds fresh out of school, Harrison realised how beneficial it could be to have time with each of them on a one-to-one basis. Youngsters were given the opportunity to discuss any issues they might have in private, without having their team-mates leaping on to any insecurities or worries they might express. He also knew he had to be frank with players about their prospects for their careers. Sometimes the news he had to impart might be disappointing, as he felt it was right to tell someone that he did not think they would be able to make the grade at United. There was no point in giving people unrealistic hopes, and it didn't mean they wouldn't be able to find another club.

On the other hand, when he told a player he had a chance to reach the first team, it usually had a galvanising effect. He remembers when he first said to Neville that he thought he had what it takes, his 'eyes nearly popped out of his head' as it gave him self-belief. Neville became a natural leader and would often be chosen to captain the side. Paul Scholes was another who Harrison felt needed his confidence reinforced, because he was small and quiet. He used other methods to inspire his players; Beckham has recalled that when he took the youth team to watch the first team in action he would say to 'watch the man playing in your position. One day, you're going to take his place.' It just planted the seed in their minds that this was what they were being groomed for.

Any praise Harrison gave seemed to his players to have been hard-earned and so was all the more valued when it came. McKee says, 'If Eric praised you, you knew you'd done well.' Casper echoes that thought: 'If you got a compliment, you knew it was well deserved.' There is no sense from any of them that they felt this approach was too harsh, and all seem to feel they benefited from Harrison's way of doing things. McKee sums it up in this way: '[We] got good life skills, and he instilled discipline and self-belief.'

Understanding how to deal with the emotional side of teenagers was one aspect of Harrison's job that was arguably more challenging than for a manager of a senior side. Another aspect was helping players deal with the changes their bodies were undergoing. For example, Beckham went through a tough time when he was 16 and 17 years old as he shot up in size – the stamina he would later become renowned for in his senior career remained, but growing so much left him short on strength. Because of this, at the start of United's Youth Cup campaign he was very much a bit-part player – it wasn't until the semi-final second leg that Beckham actually started a game. Knowing when to rest a player and understanding their physical limits is especially vital at youth-team level. Twenty years ago, getting it right was usually down to instinct and experience, compared with the modern era when everything can be much more closely monitored, thanks to the huge strides forward taken in the field of sports science. Harrison's instincts, however, were rarely wrong.

Harrison also had the problem that those he was managing were aged between 16 and 18 – just the ages when many teenagers are easily led astray by women, alcohol and any number of other distractions. We have already seen in the last chapter how the players insisted that they kept their focus on their careers and gave up much that other teenagers were enjoying. Many of them even left behind their friends during this period, not through arrogance but because they believed they could not have it all: a career and a normal teenage life. A lot of this sacrifice came from their self-motivation and dedication, but Harrison was quietly reinforcing the message all the time. He has said: 'To have talent and not to maximise it . . . is a crime.' Neville was not going to make that mistake. If he had a game on a Saturday, he would be in bed by 9.15 on Thursday and Friday nights. He adds: 'I couldn't afford even to sniff a pint of lager.' He may have been an extreme example, but the rest of them were not that different in their desire not to mess up their chances.

The other way Harrison could reinforce his mantra to the players was more direct and physical. Giggs remembers him wandering into the gym where his youth-team players were working on their fitness. While some were trying to show what they could do, Harrison quietly walked across and lifted up the entire bench-press weight machine, not just the weights. He didn't need to say much after that.

With his understanding of teenagers, his strict disciplinarian approach and his strong work ethic, Harrison knew how to get the best out of his charges. But as he himself had understood very early on, all this would get you only so far if it wasn't allied to learning how to play the game the right way and, beyond that, also coming up with the right tactics to win games. Giggs describes him as an 'excellent coach and tactician'. It was that ability that was to enable him to win the league with the 'A' team on numerous occasions while at United, even when the quality of his players wasn't always of the same standard as the Class of 92. As Beckham described it in his memoirs, 'The credit goes to him for turning us into footballers and, during the next three years, turning us into a team.' It is an assessment Casper would agree with, as he has said that Harrison was 'easily the best coach I've ever been under'.

Having won the third-round tie in the Youth Cup before Christmas, this group of kids was about to face a much more daunting task in the fourth round in February, one that would test their growing team spirit to the full. It would also shine the spotlight on them in a way they had not yet fully experienced. For next up, United were going to take on City – the pride of Manchester was at stake and, especially for the local lads in the Red shirts, this was arguably going to be the biggest match they had ever played in.

4

A Local Affair

'If you're going to be a defender, you'd better start tackling.'

Eric Harrison to Gary Neville

Fourth Round: Thursday 6 February 1992, Maine Road
Attendance: 5,500
Manchester City 1 Manchester United 3
Team: Pilkington; O'Kane, Neville, Casper, Switzer; Gillespie
(Beckham), Butt, Davies, Thornley; Burke, Savage.
Sub not used: Gordon.
Goals: O'Kane (17), Thornley (25, 75)

Whereas in the previous two rounds the coverage of United's Youth Cup run had been pretty low-key in the *Manchester Evening News,* that was never going to be the case when the city's two big clubs were drawn to face each other in the fourth round. On the day of the match itself, there was a big article in the paper looking forward to the game later that evening.

There was no doubt which side were the favourites: 'Manchester City are plotting another cup upset for their arch-rivals from Old Trafford,' the paper announced. It was 'another' one because the senior side had played a fourth-round FA Cup replay the night before at Southampton, who were languishing at the foot of the table at the time. Goals from Stuart Gray and Alan Shearer had earned the south-coast outfit a draw at the Dell, and after extra time the Reds lost a penalty shoot-out 4–2 – in the process they became the first top division side ever to go out of the FA Cup in this manner.

The paper was clear that United were 'regarded as one of the strongest sides in the country at youth level', despite the absence of Ryan Giggs, who had played in the FA Cup game the day before. With the Welshman not involved, the paper picked out two prime candidates as being the ones who were most likely to impress: 'The Reds will be looking to their promising young wingers Ben Thornley, who earned schoolboy honours with England, and Bristol-born Raphael Burke, who is a product of the FA's School of Excellence at Lilleshall.'

For the 'Boy Blues', the paper thought they would 'rely heavily on the penalty-area menace of Old Trafford-born Adrian Mike, who is the club's leading scorer at junior level'. Former Northern Ireland schoolboy international Steve Lomas was to be City's captain, while Richard Edghill was another who had been in 'sparkling form' thus far in the tournament.

A Local Affair

The paper had done a good job in picking out the City players to watch. Adie Mike, who was 13 days older than Giggs, would eventually make his first-team debut for City later in the season, and scored his first goal for the club in the final game of the campaign, as City finished the season in fifth, three places behind the Reds. Despite this spectacular start, he never quite tied down a regular place in the side and in 1995 moved on to Stockport County before being signed by Doncaster Rovers, and in 2002–03 he finished his league career at Lincoln. In total, he played 103 league games, scoring 11 goals.

Steve Lomas had easily the most successful career of any of the City side that day. The midfielder played 111 times in the league for the Blues before moving to West Ham United late in the 1996–97 season. At Upton Park he eventually became club captain and played 187 league games for the Hammers. He then moved to Queens Park Rangers and finally had a brief spell at Gillingham. He made a total of 361 league appearances and won 45 caps for Northern Ireland – many of them alongside Class of 92 star Keith Gillespie. Late in 2011, he became manager of St Johnstone after a spell in charge of West Ham Reserves.

Full-back Richard Edghill was another of the 'Boy Blues' who had a long career and, as an Oldham lad, he was one who added to the local flavour of the contest that night. He stayed at City until 2002, making 181 league appearances for them, before moving on to a series of clubs later in his career: Wigan Athletic, Sheffield United, Queens Park Rangers, Bradford City and finally Macclesfield Town. He ended his league career in 2007–08, after making 283 appearances.

Of the rest of the City side, only Rae Ingram and Jim Whitley played any league games for City. Ingram made 23 league appearances for the Blues before going on to Maccles-field Town and Port Vale, where he contracted meningitis and in 2003 found himself out of league football after making 154 career appearances.

Whitley, on the other hand, stayed at City until 2001, making just 38 league appearances for the club and often finding himself sent out on loan. In 2001, he decided to move back to the place where he had grown up – Wrexham – and had the most successful period of his career there, making 140 league appearances for the Red Dragons before retiring in 2006 following knee problems. He also won three caps for Northern Ireland.

It is worth dwelling on these achievements by United's opposition, because for a youth team to produce five players who each went on to make more than 100 league appear-ances is highly unusual, and it shows that, even if United went into the game as favourites, there was plenty of real talent in the City side, too.

While the game was a true Manchester derby, with lots of local lads in action, for Whitley and Robbie Savage this was a return to their school days. When Whitley moved to the UK from Zambia, his family settled in Wrexham and he continued his education at Ysgol Bryn Alyn. In the mid-1980s, there were very few black people in the Welsh town and Whitley found himself the target of abuse from some of the pupils. Savage stepped in to stop it getting out of hand and the two began a friendship that continues to this day.

A Local Affair

The two boys didn't just enjoy playing football and other sports together. Savage credits Whitley with helping him secure his seven GCSEs, as he spent most of the exams looking across at Whitley's answers and copying them down. Savage even helped his friend get a trial at Manchester City, so when the two lined up against each other that night at Maine Road it was with the friendliest of rivalries – not that either of them was likely to hold back in any way.

Of course, it was not unusual at this stage of their careers for players in Youth Cup games to find themselves coming up against people they had played with or against in their school days. But a derby match was going to be especially significant. George Switzer recalls how he knew at least two or three of his opponents from his schoolboy football days playing for Salford Boys.

One member of the United line-up was always up for the challenge when it came to taking on the Reds' biggest rivals: Gary Neville. By the time the derby came along, he had blossomed in confidence. Youth-team manager Eric Harrison explains: 'I must admit when I first saw him, I thought: "No, he's not first-team material." Twelve years of age and I didn't think so. Thirteen – great improvement, but probably still not. But when he got to fourteen, fifteen, I thought: "You know, I've made a mistake in my judgement here." At sixteen years of age, I made him my youth-team captain.'

As Harrison's comments reveal, it had not been an easy journey for Neville to get this far. He was born in Bury, a few miles north of Manchester, on 18 February 1975 and by the time he was four his father was taking him to Old Trafford to watch United. His early heroes included Bryan Robson,

Mark Hughes and Norman Whiteside. He was fortunate to be born into a naturally talented sporting family, with both his parents being keen amateurs, but it was to be Gary and his younger twin siblings, Phil and Tracey, who would make a huge success of it. Between them they won 218 England caps, with Tracey picking up 74 of them for netball, while Gary (85) and Phil (59) shared the rest.

There's a famous 'sledge' in cricket that took place when Mark Waugh saw James Ormond coming out to bat for England in 2001. In typically blunt antipodean language, Waugh spoke out: 'What are you doing out here? There's no way you're good enough to play for England.' There may have been one or two other words in there as well.

Immediately, looking in the direction of Waugh's brother Steve, captain of Australia, Ormond shot back with: 'Maybe not, but at least I'm the best player in my family.'

When one reads his autobiography, there is a sense that, even though he was the big brother, Gary felt Phil was the better all-round player: 'Teams wanted me; they begged to have Phil.' They would play football or cricket as much as possible on a local field known as the Barracks. Phil was an early developer, playing above his age group and for England Schoolboys (something Gary never did). So, Gary recalls in his memoirs, 'I had a younger brother keeping me on my toes and he had a bigger brother to topple.'

The combination and fraternal rivalry drove both of them on, as did the hard work of their lorry driver father, who passed on the valuable lesson that you only get out of life what you put in. Phil was on his way through the United junior ranks, too, and would form part of the Youth Cup squad in 1992–93, even though he was still just 15 when they began their defence of the title. Indeed, Phil remembers his father's influence having an impact from the first time he went to watch United in action. The Reds were taking on Aston Villa, and he recalls his father pointing out Mike Duxbury, who played in Phil's position, and saying: 'Look! That's what you've got to do.' Clearly, there was no lack of ambition in the Neville household.

Gary went to Chantlers Primary School in the west of Bury, and found most of the pupils there were Liverpool supporters – a new rivalry was born. Without doubt he showed promise, and one day, he remembers: 'My primary school teacher came up to me and told me he'd nominated me for a trial and I went to the trial at Littleton Road with about 160 kids. Sixteen were selected, and I don't know how I was selected – it just seemed to be millions of little kids running around the field, but fortunately for me someone spotted something.'

So in 1986, at the age of 11, Neville was playing at United's Centre of Excellence at the Cliff. He was taken there by his father every Monday and Thursday – for him, it was a 'hallowed place'. Originally a midfielder, he saw how the quality of his rivals was increasing as the club's net widened, especially when Nicky Butt and Paul Scholes joined a couple of years later. Butt was 'as hard as nails . . . he was intimidating', while Scholes, though small and asthmatic, had obvious talent. They had come from Boundary Park, the best junior side in the region, whereas he played for Bury Juniors. 'I fell a long way short [of their ability],' he remembers. To keep up with them, he decided to join them there in the hope that this would help his game. Phil also made the move to the Oldham outfit.

At 14 came the first key moment in his career: would he be given schoolboy terms by United? He was thrilled when he was not only given a two-year deal as a schoolboy, but also two years as a YTS apprentice to follow when he reached 16 – now Neville knew he had four years to prove himself worthy to be a United player. But meanwhile the quality of the competition he had to beat continued to improve: Ben Thornley was now a part of the set-up and seemed to be equally as good with his left foot as with his right. For Neville, however well he got on with his mates at the club, he also knew they were rivals of his, and that he needed to find an edge if he was to have a chance.

Neville felt well supported at home, of course, with his parents rarely missing the opportunity to come to watch him play, but also at the Cliff, where Brian Kidd's presence as head of Academy was reassuring. He found Harrison a 'scary Yorkshireman', and even at 14 he often found his training sessions being supervised by Archie Knox, Ferguson's assistant. 'The intensity was incredible,' he recalls. It was another way that the club let their youngsters know they were part of something bigger: the man who coached England and United captain Bryan Robson was also making time to teach them a few things.

During the school holidays, the local lads were joined by David Beckham from London, Keith Gillespie from Northern Ireland and Robbie Savage from Wales, among others. Yet again, the bar was raised, and Neville found himself being edged out of the side to make way for them. He fell back on his work ethic and his organisational skills and hoped they would see him through.

Fortunately for him, his development had been noted by Harrison, and when he reached 16 he was kept on as an apprentice. But with competition so fierce in the midfield, Neville moved back into central defence. It was a change of approach for him, as in those days he felt his strengths were as a ball player, but Harrison had some words of advice: 'If you're going to be a defender, you'd better start tackling.' And so it was that Neville found himself at centre-back against Sunderland in the second round of the Youth Cup, his first important game in that role, and came through well. Finally, he began to develop the vital element of self-belief that would make all the difference to his career. From now on, his progress would be rapid.

Gary's presence at United confirmed to Phil that this was where he wanted his future to lie, not in cricket. (Phil was a hugely promising young cricketer, who was coming through the Lancashire ranks at the same time as Andrew Flintoff – the county reckoned Neville was the better prospect at that stage.) When Phil started as an apprentice, his elder brother was able to give him useful tips on how to keep on the right side of Harrison. He also picked up from his brother the need 'to make sacrifices such as not going out late'. Knowing that their lives would be restricted in this way helped all the players to bond socially, because those who hadn't got a football career to prepare for felt free to go out when they wanted.

Ben Thornley was another local lad who lined up for United in the derby match. Born in Bury on 21 April 1975, he was a couple of months younger than Neville (and was actually born in the same hospital as him, Fairfield), but as we have seen was already tipped as one of the brightest prospects in the Class of 92.

He'd moved from Bury to Eccles as a small boy – his father was a headmaster and his work had taken him to West Salford. Thornley began his education at Clarendon Road Junior School, before moving on to Ellesmere Park High School and then Wentworth High School. By the time he reached secondary school, he was already making an impression as a player, and his father (then headmaster at Cadishead School) was instrumental in getting him to join Cadishead FC, where a lot of the pupils played at the weekend.

In his third year at secondary school, he started playing for Salford Boys and because of his talent was lifted up an age group so he could play in the same side as Giggs and Switzer. He recalls how Salford made it all the way to the national final of one competition, where they met St Helens at Old Trafford. By now various clubs were interested in signing him up, and he was invited for a trial at Ipswich Town. But for Thornley there was only ever one club he wanted to play for, and he was prepared to wait for United to come for him. Because of this, he never signed associate schoolboy forms with any other club. Meanwhile, his father realised that football was in danger of taking over Thornley's life (he was playing virtually every day), so he made sure he didn't forget his studies. 'His advice was always sound,' says the winger.

Despite his wish to join United, if it hadn't been for the manager, he might very well have been playing against United in the Youth Cup fourth round. He recalls what happened: 'I was actually at Manchester City at the time. I think I must have been one of the very few privileged kids who had Alex Ferguson round to the house with Brian Kidd one Friday evening to talk to myself and my parents, and obviously when I knew that he was interested it swayed my decision, and I went with my heart and went there.' In truth, with Salford Boys playing their games about 50 yards from the Cliff, United's scouts did not have far to go to see his potential, and Thornley suspects he was watched on many occasions by the club before they contacted him.

Because of his previous links with City, Thornley remembers that a friend of his at the club, Joe Liddiat, kept on warning him that the City full-back was going to kick him up in the air every time he got the ball. The winger laughed and told him that the defender would have to catch him first. Although it was a derby, with all that that meant, there was still time for a joke.

Perhaps unsurprisingly, Thornley and Neville were close friends, and remain in touch to this day. They were often joined by Chris Casper and David Beckham, and the four of them even went on holiday together to Malta – as the latter recalls, it was a lads' holiday but they didn't do anything 'you'd need to keep a secret from your mum'.

They would also go to Johnsons in the centre of Manchester for a night out most Wednesdays. Thornley seemed the most outgoing, while Neville was always worried that they would get caught up in some trouble and would not relax until he felt safe. Somewhat surprisingly, given that one of their number would go on to become a global sex symbol, in those days it was Thornley (nicknamed 'Squeaky' because of his voice) and not Beckham who attracted the girls. Most times, they would end up going back to Thornley's family house for the night, which left three of them shivering on the floor in the lounge while Thornley was tucked up in his own bed.

As we have seen, Thornley had made the biggest impact at the start of the season, when he had inspired United to the Milk Cup in Northern Ireland. He had scored in the third round of the Youth Cup and was developing into a superb winger, with pace, strength and great ability.

Behind Thornley on the left flank that evening was George Switzer, the Salford lad who played at left-back. Born on 13 October 1973, Switzer was one of the oldest members of the squad and was an all-action full-back, just as capable of rampaging forward to set up an attack as he was of stopping them at the other end. A stocky, ginger-haired lad, he gave his all to the cause.

Switzer was another, like Neville, who was scooped up very early by United and asked to come and train at the club. Initially, he just went along with some of his friends to watch them play, but then got involved himself. Soon it developed into something a little more formal. He remembers: 'I was just playing for my local Sunday team, Barr Hill, and for my school, and got a call from my headmaster at St Joseph's saying there's a letter here from Man United. I didn't have a clue what it was; it just said would you like to come down to the School of Excellence. I just went from there. I thought it was one of my mates winding me up, or my brother having a laugh.'

St Joseph's in Ordsall was about a mile away up Trafford Road from Old Trafford, while Barr Hill was a Salford boys' football club that had been established in 1944 and was renowned as one of the best in the area at that time. Given that he lived so close to Old Trafford, it was not surprising that United picked him up so early, for as Giggs has commented: 'He was an unbelievable player when he was ten, eleven.' Because the two of them were invariably the best players in their school sides in those days, Switzer would usually be given the task of marking Giggs. It must have been as good a way to learn the defender's art as any other, though both of them often played in the centre of midfield at that stage of their careers, so they could have maximum impact on a game.

Switzer recalls his early days at United: 'When I first started it was Ron Atkinson, and I never saw him once; he never came down and trained us. But as soon as the gaffer, Alex, took over, him and Archie Knox were down there every training session. I couldn't wait to get home from school, get ready and my dad would take me down. Just amazing! I already knew Ryan then. We played for Salford Under-11s – that's how I knew him. Plus from school – we used to play against each other for school.'

This was Switzer's second season in the Youth Cup side, and he remembers how, as this game drew near, and as the United side continued their run towards the final, he would hear people on the streets of his home area say to him: 'Come on, do it for Salford, son!' There were many from the Greater Manchester area in the United side, but it's fair to say that Switzer was the most local of all the squad, and as such he was always one of the most popular players in the team with the fans. He was living the dream and now was the chance to take the next step to making it a reality.

But to do that, first Switzer had to help United overcome the Blues. City's youth-team manager Terry Darracott, who had spent over a decade playing for Everton, knew his United counterpart Harrison well from his time at the Toffees. It was just one more battle of wits that the Blues boss was looking forward to. He said: 'Tonight's match should be a cracker. All derby games are fiercely contested because there is so much local pride at stake and that applies to the juniors every bit as much as the seniors.'

For the game, City opened up the Main Stand at their ground and a crowd of almost 5,500, paying £2 each for an adult and £1 for a junior, came to see what would transpire in this repeat of the 1986 Youth Cup final. With four local lads in the side – Butt, Neville, Switzer and Thornley – United had plenty of players who knew all about how much was at stake.

One man who nearly didn't make it to see the game was Tony Pilkington, Kevin's father. As United's goalkeeper that night recalls, his father didn't know the way to Maine Road, having travelled over from Nottinghamshire, and got lost down a quiet side street. Fortunately, he saw a group of young women standing on the corner, so he rolled down the window to ask for directions. It was only then that he noticed they weren't dressed entirely appropriately for a cold February evening and soon realised they were offering a little bit more than a local geography lesson. He made a suitably swift exit and got to the ground just in time.

There were a few changes to the line-up compared with the previous two rounds. Chris Casper came into the centre of defence alongside Neville, which meant that John O'Kane moved across to right-back and Mark Gordon slipped out of the side and on to the bench. Burke came into the side to replace Colin McKee, and Beckham regained his place on the bench with Giggs not available. With Burke, Gillespie and Thornley all in the side, United had a surfeit of wingers but were short of out-and-out strikers. However, with so much pace in the side, they were sure to be a threat to City.

Darracott was proved right about the game, as Paul Hince reported the following day in the *Manchester Evening News*. Under the heading 'United Babes in the Mood', he described the clash as a 'pulsating' match. Once again, as in previous rounds, United were quick to establish a grip on the game. The first goal, after 17 minutes, came from the unlikely source of John O'Kane, who put the ball into the net from close range. He had been set up by Savage, who had beaten the offside trap, but was clattered by the keeper before he could finish. On 25 minutes, a poor back pass from Nev Riches was intercepted by Thornley, who was again reported to be 'impressive', and he then took the ball round the stranded City keeper Richard Bibby to give the Reds a 2–0 lead.

City didn't let their heads go down. Hince wrote how the goal 'sparked a spirited revival inspired by their driving skipper Steve Lomas'. Five minutes later, they were back in the game after Adie Mike's superb run down the right wing. He sent over an excellent cross and Scott Thomas was there to head home. The score remained 2–1 until 15 minutes from time when Thornley decided the outcome after he cut in from the left wing and blasted the ball into the bottom corner of the net.

After the game a delighted Ferguson commented: 'Both sets of kids did their clubs proud, but we took control in the second half and were worthy winners in the end.' City manager Peter Reid admitted as much when he said: 'United were just too strong for us. I thought we were in with a chance at half time, but they dominated after the interval.'

The Class of 92 had come through their biggest test to date in front of a crowd that was on a par with the average in Division Three (now League One) that season. With the levels of expectation growing, Harrison took the decision to try to keep the core of the Youth Cup side together for 'A' team games, so the squad could be familiar with each other. Fortunately, they didn't have long to wait for the next round, for just a week later they were due to be in action in the quarter-final. Having won local bragging rights, their next opponents were from Merseyside, another area that has supplied some traditional rivalry for the Reds. But this time it wasn't Liverpool or Everton that United would face, but Tranmere Rovers. If they could beat them, they'd be just one step away from the final.

5

The Fledglings Take to the Wing

'I didn't understand the discipline, the mental strength that was needed.'

Raphael Burke

Fifth Round: Thursday 13 February 1992, Old Trafford
Attendance: 8,708
Manchester United 2 Tranmere Rovers 0
Team: Pilkington; O'Kane, Switzer, Casper, Neville; McKee (Beckham), Butt, Davies, Thornley (Burke); Giggs, Savage.
Goals: Giggs (40, 60)

With United's first team not due to have a game the following Saturday, having been knocked out of the FA Cup in the previous round, the good news for the Reds' Youth Cup prospects was that it gave their manager Eric Harrison a chance to field Ryan Giggs from the start for the first time in their campaign. Having the young Welshman in their ranks was a huge boost to their chances in what was predicted to be a tough encounter against Tranmere Rovers. The Merseysiders had already beaten Liverpool and Oldham Athletic (the conquerors of Leeds United, whose senior side would win the league title this season) to get to this stage, so they were definitely not a side to be underestimated.

Giggs was one of two changes to the starting line-up from the previous round, with Colin McKee returning to the team after missing the previous game. Raphael Burke and Keith Gillespie were the two to make way for them. For Burke, there was at least the consolation of a place on the bench, where he was joined by David Beckham, but for Gillespie his participation in the Youth Cup run was now all but over.

Giggs was the player who had been getting the bulk of the media coverage throughout United's Youth Cup run to date, despite having played for just ten minutes of the campaign. He continued to be the centre of attention this time as well, as the *Manchester Evening News* match report was headlined: 'Red Kids Make it so Easy for Giggs'. Of course, we all now know what the future held for him, but early in 1992 he was still just a glittering prospect who had had a dramatic early impact at first-team level; no one could be completely sure that he would go on to fulfil his obvious potential.

He had been born in Cardiff on 29 November 1973 and was named Ryan Joseph Wilson. His mother, Lynne, was a children's nurse and cook, while his father, Danny, was a rugby player who played top-level union as a fly-half for Cardiff. Both his parents were still in their teens when Ryan was born, and their relationship was a turbulent one. As a young boy, he would often go to stay with his grandparents, where he was assured of a calmer environment than was sometimes possible at home.

That support network was taken away from Ryan in 1980, when Wilson was offered a contract to change rugby codes and to go to play rugby league for Swinton. In those days, rugby union was still an amateur sport, which made life difficult for those who wanted to devote their time to the game. Instead, training and matches had to be fitted around their other work. Wilson played outside-half for his new club, a mid-table Second Division side attracting about 2,000 fans on average to a league game. He was a smooth-running half-back, and clips of him in action reveal that he had superb natural balance, often able to keep his feet in a challenge when others would go to ground. It was a gift he would pass on to his son.

The year after changing codes, he won three of his four Wales caps, as his career seemed to be developing well. But tensions remained at home, and Ryan found himself in that horrible position, caught between his warring parents. In 1985 and 1987, Wilson helped Swinton win promotion to the First Division, but on each occasion they were relegated back down after one year. In January 1988, he moved to Springfield Borough, a smaller club, and not long after that retired from the game.

In those days, Swinton were based in Station Road, Pendlebury, in Salford, not very far north from where George Switzer was to be found in action at Barr Hill. Ryan went to Grosvenor Road Primary School, about a mile away from the ground, and then at the age of 11 he moved on to Moorside

High School, which was a little further out, along the East Lancashire Road.

Given his father's profession, it was not surprising that the young Ryan Wilson was much in demand to play rugby league at school. Until the age of 14, he was attached to Salford Boys and Langworthy rugby league clubs, the latter based in Oakwood Park. But he was also a natural talent at football, playing for Salford Boys (who, as we have seen, would play at the Cliff) and on Sunday mornings for Deans FC. His mother was a regular on the touchline, giving him support all the way. He was captain of the Salford side when they beat Blackburn at Anfield in 1987 to win the Granada Cup, and by now football scouts were beginning to take notice of him.

By the time he had reached his teens, it was becoming increasingly clear to him that his physique was more likely to lend itself to him playing football rather than rugby league. And when Deans coach Dennis Schofield, a scout for Manchester City, took him along to that club for some trials, Ryan Wilson knew which sport was going to be the one for him.

Having said that, he confessed in his memoirs that he 'absolutely hated it' there, as he was a United fan, and it just did not feel right to him to be playing for the club's fiercest rivals. Fortunately, this was where fate stepped in to change the course of his life, not to mention the history of Manchester United. Harold Wood, an Old Trafford steward who ran a local newsagent's, was a regular supporter of Deans, and he kept on writing to Alex Ferguson to say there was a special player he should come to have a look at who was right on his doorstep. As we saw earlier on, in his first months in charge of United, Ferguson was anxious to sign up any local talent he could find to send out a message to the entire city that United was the club to go to.

Giggs recalls that his first trial at United took place over the Christmas holidays in 1986, and after that the club kept a close eye on him. At first sight, Ferguson believed he was a 'certainty' to make it. So, on 29 November 1987, Wilson's 14th birthday, Ferguson came to his house, bringing with him Joe Brown, and offered him a two-year deal as an associate schoolboy. Wilson had had other approaches, and United's offer was not the best – but it was from the club he wanted to join. And that was enough. He signed up immediately.

Once he joined United, his progress was spectacular. He was soon playing for England Schoolboys, and manager Dave Bushell even made him captain. Then, at 15, after his parents separated, he decided to take his mother's maiden name as his surname, and England Schoolboy international Ryan Wilson became the young Welsh winger Ryan Giggs, as he decided to revert to his family roots in Wales as far as his international career was concerned. Although many have lamented the Giggs-sized hole on England's left flank for much of the last 20 years, the man himself has always been clear where his roots were.

With his father gone, times were very tough at home and money was in short supply; they had metered electricity and no central heating to keep the place warm. Once he started to receive his apprentice pay of £29.50, he made sure that he handed over his wages to his mother to help out with the bills. Unlike most of his fellow youth-teamers, Giggs had a steady girlfriend at the time, Sue, and they went out together for four years until he was 19. For much of that period, although they would often go to the pub on their nights out, Giggs was still too young to drink.

Giggs was progressing rapidly at United as well, lining up for the Reserves while still just 15 and taking his chance against the seniors. More usually, he was in action for the 'B' and 'A' sides, as well as in the Youth Cup, where United reached the semi-finals in both 1990 and 1991. In the summer of 1990, he began his formal apprenticeship, but as the 1990–91 season wore on it became clear to all those in charge that the 17-year-old was ready for the next step.

Eventually, on 2 March 1991, he found himself on the bench for United's first team as they took on Everton at Old Trafford in front of 45,656 fans. When Denis Irwin had to come off, Giggs made his official debut as a United player, lining up as a forward alongside Danny Wallace. The Reds were already 2–0 down at the time, falling behind to goals from Mike Newell and Dave Watson, and Giggs could do nothing to turn things round.

He had to wait a couple of months to make his first start for the senior side, but Ferguson had no qualms about throwing him into one of the most intense games possible: against Manchester City, the club who had first given him a trial. It could not have gone better for him, as the young star scored the only goal of the match. Had United not taken just one point from their final three matches (without Giggs), it would have ensured the Blues did not finish above their Manchester neighbours that season. If United's local rivals were cursing themselves at having let him slip from their grasp that day, the pain was only going to increase over the next two decades and more.

Being a boy among men could have been a daunting experience for him, but Giggs recalls that fellow Welshmen Mark Hughes and Clayton Blackmore backed him up whenever he was on the receiving end of too much banter from his teammates. Meanwhile, on the pitch any player who tried to physically intimidate him was warned off from doing so by skipper Bryan Robson. It was a message only the most foolhardy would have ignored. Off the pitch, Ferguson kept him away from the media as much as possible, though they were all desperate to hear from the teenage sensation. In this safe environment, Giggs was given the opportunity to blossom as a player and as a person.

But while the club wrapped him up in a protective cocoon as far as the outside world was concerned, within the confines of Old Trafford they were working on making sure he could handle whatever was thrown at him. And Eric Harrison made sure he received the full force of his motivational methods. In his memoirs, the youth-team manager recalls how he once took an Under-18 side to a tournament in Italy with the 15-year-old Giggs among their number. Harrison had been working with him on improving his right foot, and had also often played him as centre-forward, so that he would be in the game more and could improve his running off the ball. During one game on the tour, Harrison felt Giggs was not performing to the level expected of him and at half time gave the young Welshman a major roasting. After he'd finished, Brian Kidd had a quiet word, suggesting that Harrison might have been too harsh on him, especially as he was so young. Eric replied that Giggs would very soon be in the first team, and he would face much worse then, so he'd better get used to it now. Preparing a player for the senior side wasn't simply a matter of giving them the right coaching – they had to be able to take a good old-fashioned managerial blast as well.

Because his rise to the first team was so meteoric, Giggs now feels that he might have benefited from having longer in the junior ranks, where there is more time to work on basic skills, as Harrison tried to do. For, once a player is in the first-team squad, the emphasis of training changes and mastery of the basic skills is deemed to be a given for anyone good enough to reach that level. This meant he would have to iron out any weaknesses in his game on his own. Just imagine what he might have been like if he'd managed to develop his full potential! Despite the fear that he might have lacked the final degree of polish to his game, by 1991–92, as Gary Neville says, '[He] was the one everyone looked up to, because he was on a different level to us in terms of skill, speed; in terms of experience he was unbelievable.'

Given the belief of his team-mates and the press that Giggs could pretty much win the game on his own, it perhaps comes as little surprise that both of United's goals against Tranmere were scored by the first-teamer. But as *Manchester Evening News* writer David Meek was quick to report after the match: 'Don't run away with the idea that the United youngsters are a one-man team.'

The main credit for the first goal, which came five minutes before the interval, should really have gone to Ben Thornley. The move began when Nicky Butt broke up play in the centre of midfield with a superb tackle. He moved the ball out to Thornley on the wing, who surged forward, cut inside and beat the keeper with a low shot. It would surely have crossed the line anyway, but Giggs was on hand to poke it over to give the Reds a 1–0 lead at the break.

Giggs scored again 15 minutes into the second half when Simon Davies (who had handed the captain's armband to the star man) sent over a cross that just needed to be converted. He was never going to miss the opportunity. In what was arguably their most complete performance in the competition to date, the Reds were denied further goals only by the superb form of Tranmere's keeper Danny Coyne.

Coyne won't have appreciated being beaten twice by a fellow Welshman. Three months older than Giggs, he would make his league debut for Rovers the following season and would stay with the club until 1999, making more than a hundred league appearances for them. It was at his next club, Grimsby Town, that he had his most regular football, missing just three league games in four seasons. In the summer of 2003, he moved to Championship side Leicester City, where he joined Keith Gillespie (though they played together only once, in the Carling Cup), the man who had been edged out of the Youth Cup side by Giggs. Unable to displace Ian Walker from the starting line-up, Coyne went to Burnley in 2004, before returning to Tranmere for a couple of seasons and then in 2009 heading to Middlesbrough.

A consistent and talented keeper at all but the very highest level, Coyne won 16 caps for Wales and made his debut for his country on the same day as United's Davies – in a 2–0 defeat to Switzerland in Lugano on 24 April 1996. Robbie

Savage won his second Wales cap in the same fixture. During the 2011–12 season, when he was one of the very few players from that Youth Cup campaign still to be in league action, Coyne made the 500th first-class appearance of his career. He is working on his coaching badges now, and has been helping out with Boro's Academy side – bringing him back to where his own career started.

But the game wasn't all about Coyne's heroics. Tranmere boss Warwick Rimmer had put together an excellent team, and they made sure the Reds knew they'd been in a contest. In fact, he was the man largely responsible for the club even being in the competition at all, as he had set up a new youth policy as recently as 1987. Before then, the youth programme had been cut owing to financial pressures, but chairman Peter Johnson knew how important it was to be strong at junior level, and in Rimmer he found the right man for the job. With almost 20 years as a player behind him, at Bolton Wanderers and Crewe Alexandra, he had all the experience and know-how to help his club compete at youth level with the big boys on Merseyside. Beating Liverpool earlier in the campaign was for that reason especially gratifying.

United youth manager Harrison acknowledged how difficult it had been to win the tie: 'Everyone warned me that we would be in for a hard game and they were right. I thought it was going to be one of those nights when we would never score. Their goalkeeper was saving everything and I think it inspired them to hit back hard. But we played some decent football and I was pleased with everyone's performance. I think we have some very useful players in this season's team. They have good futures if they keep working at it.'

The Fledglings Take to the Wing

Even though United were now in the semi-final of the Youth Cup, Harrison was clearly not going to get too excited or start making rash promises. After all, he'd reached this stage and got no further the previous two seasons. But it was a sign of just how much the United fans were getting behind the team that the 8,708 crowd for this game was 60 per cent higher than it had been for the derby a week before. Obviously, Giggs was a part of that appeal, but the message was out: these kids were a little bit special.

While his opposite number had been getting much of the attention because of his heroics at the other end, United's keeper Kevin Pilkington was celebrating his first clean sheet of the cup run. He was born in Hitchin, Hertfordshire, on 8 March 1974 and moved to the East Midlands when he was about five years old. Although his father had had trials for Notts County in his youth, there was no real sporting pedigree in his family. Despite that, 'Dad loved coming to watch me play and took me everywhere, all over the country, to help out.'

Pilkington went to Swanwick Hall School in Alfreton and played in goal for them, even though it wasn't until he reached the age of 14 that he really shot up in height. He also played for the local village side as well, but got his break when Harrowby United in Grantham were short of a keeper one day and asked if he would step in. From there, he graduated to playing county football.

Soon he was on the radar of United's Midlands scouts. Ray Medwell contacted his parents, Tony and Eileen, to let them know he was coming to watch Kevin in action, as he thought there might be an opportunity for him at the club.

As Pilkington remembers, 'To be fair, it's one of the best games I've ever played, so it was one of those lucky things. I did well, so they said come up for a trial for a few weeks. So I went up, played a few games, did OK and they said they'd sign me.'

The truth was, according to Harrison, that the club was desperate to find a keeper at youth level and had put out an 'SOS' to all the scouts to see who they could unearth. For some reason, the club had consistently struggled to find good young keepers at that time since Gary Walsh in 1986. When they approached him, Pilkington was still in college and was the only member of the Youth Cup side who was yet to sign professional forms at the club, though he would do so at the end of the season. He'd barely arrived at United – playing just three games for the 'B' team, the first of them on the artificial pitch at Preston North End – before he was taking his place in the Youth Cup side against Sunderland at the start of the cup run. His form had been so good that he had even been picked for the England Schools Under-18 side. Perhaps because it had all happened so fast for him, he was known as one of the quieter members of the group and had to suffer with the nickname 'Doofer'. He recalls that it was fellow-apprentice Sean McAuley who came up with the tag, and to this day he has no idea why, but even his brother Gareth now calls him by that name.

While the last few months had been something of a blur for Pilkington, there was another member of the team whose career seemed to have been mapped out for a while. Raphael Burke was a right-sided midfielder who had made his England Schoolboys debut as long ago as 1988 and went on to win 13 caps at junior level. He was born in Bristol on 3 July 1974, and was educated at Merrywood School in Knowle. He played for local side Avon Athletic, one of the most successful junior clubs in the Southwest, and was invited to the local British Airways centre of excellence. There he showed such promise that he went to the FA's Academy at Lilleshall, where he spent a couple of years between 1988 and 1990.

Within a month of finishing at Lilleshall, he had moved up from Bristol to join United, becoming an apprentice in July 1990. Although he'd had the experience of life with the FA school, he found things very different at the Cliff: 'Expectations are massive and at Manchester United – you can't have a bad day. My character was developed by being at such a brilliantly run club.'

Although there was plenty of talent in his year group, headed of course by Giggs, Burke was aware that those in the year below were a formidable bunch – and not just on the football field. The second-year apprentices would regularly try to put their juniors in their place and make the most of their seniority. However, one lad was having none of it when Burke tried to impose this natural order of things. Nicky Butt was never going to let anyone take advantage of him. 'He'd have me in a headlock – it was mess-about banter,' recalls Burke. The newcomers could take care of themselves in every sense of the word, and he adds, 'It's a privilege to have played with such a good bunch.'

Burke's early highlights in his career were beginning to be put into context. In his position as a right-sided midfielder, he was competing not just to replace the first-team incumbent, Andrei Kanchelskis, but also with Beckham and Gillespie.

Many wide men are equally adept on either wing, but on the left Giggs and Lee Sharpe were already in contention, while within the youth ranks Thornley was widely regarded as one of the brightest prospects. As Gary Neville had worked out, if you were going to stay on as part of the United set-up, you needed to find a gap to fill so you could make yourself as indispensable as possible. Unfortunately for Burke, everywhere he looked there were people blocking his way forward.

Burke's chances of progress were undoubtedly hampered by the rapidly developing Beckham, who increasingly became seen as the more likely player to succeed. This was particularly true when, as Robbie Savage describes it, Burke was 'inconsistently brilliant'. Davies echoes that assessment, saying he was 'technically the best, but struggled to keep up with the rest'. The natural ability that he had did not always shine through. This was particularly damaging, as one of the key factors in deciding which players were suited to a professional career was that they should perform to a consistently high standard. Burke would make one more appearance, as a substitute in the first leg of the semi-final, before he found himself edged out of the Youth Cup side. So the one who had been seen as the star player, when Giggs joined United at 14, was now struggling to get into the side.

Burke would accept the validity of Savage's comment. He himself admits, 'I didn't deserve to play in the final – I knew I wasn't playing well and I couldn't work out how to.' Confidence was an issue, he feels, and however hard Harrison and his team tried to work on that, in the end 'that has to come from within you'. He also recognises that the thing that set some of the others apart from him was that 'I didn't understand the discipline, the mental strength that was needed' to play at the highest level. In short, he realises that those who achieved a successful football career deserved it more than he did, because their work-rate and discipline were better than his. This honest assessment of where he didn't quite match up is delivered without bitterness or regret, but with an understanding that sometimes people's lives take them down different pathways.

Burke's story also highlights one of the reasons why youth-team football appeals to so many people: its sheer uncertainty. Of the 17 players who appeared in United's Youth Cup run that season, only four of them would never make an official league appearance. If you'd have asked his fellow apprentices in the autumn of 1991, few would have chosen Burke to be among the unlucky ones. He seemed to have all the natural talent required to make it, but on its own that is rarely enough. Players must also have a capacity, and even enthusiasm, for hard work. He recognises now that he could have worked harder then. However, beyond that, apprentices are also gaining in strength as they mature, learning how to perform to a consistently high standard and understanding the responsibilities of their role in the team. The more of this they pick up, the closer they will be to becoming the complete package. It is a lot to take on in a short period – the world of professional football is a results-driven business that cannot afford to wait too long. Because of this, some players hit their ceiling very early on, while others have the priceless ability to go on improving. The football careers of Giggs and Burke show how quickly the paths can diverge, even between the ages of 14 and 18.

For Harrison's team, it was getting to the stage of the Youth Cup campaign now where it was vital that they continued to improve, as their next opponents were Tottenham Hotspur, and in their ranks were two of the English game's most promising young talents: Nick Barmby and Sol Campbell, both of whom had played alongside Burke at Lilleshall and were tipped for great things. Many reckoned that Spurs had the best young side in the country. Could United beat them and make their way through to Harrison's third Youth Cup final since he arrived at Old Trafford?

6

That's Sol, Folks

'Hard work supplies its own reward.'

Colin Savage

Semi-final, First Leg: Saturday 7 March 1992, Old Trafford
Attendance: 7,633
Manchester United 3 Tottenham Hotspur 0
Team: Pilkington; O'Kane, Neville, Casper, Switzer; McKee (Burke), Butt, Davies (Beckham), Thornley; Giggs, Savage.
Goals: Jordan (7, og), Giggs (11, 23)

Semi-final, Second Leg: Wednesday 25 March 1992, White Hart Lane
Tottenham Hotspur 1 Manchester United 2
Team: Pilkington; O'Kane, Neville, Casper, Switzer; Beckham, Butt, Davies, Thornley (Taylor); McKee, Savage (Roberts).
Goals: Butt (16), Thornley (17)

After disappointments at the semi-final stage of the competition in the last two years, Eric Harrison was anxious to
avoid another slip-up. This time, however, he had good
reason for feeling more confident. His first-year apprentices
had progressed extremely well throughout the season and
now provided the bulk of the side. Their temperament was
sound, so he believed they would cope well with the pressure
of the situation. All the players knew how much the FA
Youth Cup meant to United, to Alex Ferguson and to
Harrison, but they felt ready for the contest.

For the first time, Harrison picked an unchanged side from
the previous round and ensured his charges were well prepared for the task ahead. Two years ago, the same opposition
had stood in his way, and it was United who had gone out.
He was also aware that Tottenham Hotspur had defeated
Everton 4–0 to get to the semi-final, and in their run to this
stage they had scored 18 goals and conceded just one. No
wonder he said ahead of the game, 'They are a strong side as
well as a skilful one and we will have all our work cut out getting through to the final.'

The *Manchester Evening News* was also cautious about
United's prospects: 'The Reds will do well to go through
because they have a particularly youthful team. Ryan Giggs is
still eligible and he played in the last-round win over
Tranmere, but they are short of experience, with their goalkeeper still at school.' While picking out Kevin Pilkington as
a potential weak link may have been a little harsh, the point
about United's overall inexperience was well made.

Robbie Savage was one of those first-years still feeling his
way. Born on 18 October 1974, he grew up in Pine Close,

Bradley, on the outskirts of Wrexham. Like many of his team-mates, he was a football-mad kid who spent his childhood playing in the local park, usually against bigger children – many of them the friends of his brother Jonathan, who was three years older than him. He would often have to be dragged away from the field by his parents when it was teatime or there was homework to be done.

His first club was Llay United, which had been founded as recently as 1980. As an 11-year-old, he was a prolific striker for the club, scoring 74 goals in 28 games in one season. His form was good enough for him to be picked up by the Wrexham District side, and it was while he was playing for them against Crewe Alexandra that he got his first major break. Barry Burnell, who ran Crewe's School of Excellence, was impressed with his performance and invited him to come to join the club just before Savage's 13th birthday.

Meanwhile, Savage's father Colin, a sales manager, had decided to set up a boys' team in Wrexham, and inevitably Robbie was a part of the Bradley Youth side. By the end of the 1987–88 season, things were going very well for him: at Crewe, manager Dario Gradi gave him a glowing report on his performances that campaign, while back in Wales he continued to perform very well for both Wrexham Schoolboys and Bradley. And it was in Wales where local United scout Hugh Roberts came to see him play.

Savage takes up the story of what happened next: 'He spoke to my dad after the game. It was a funny story because my dad was cleaning up the kit, being the manager, and my mum came in and said there's a fellah wants to speak to you outside. "Well, tell him to go away, I'm too busy" – and it was a Man U scout! But he spoke to him in the end.'

So it was that in August 1988 Joe Brown asked Savage to come up to Manchester for trials. He was one of 33 young hopefuls who stayed in halls of residence in Salford University for the duration of the trial. Even though it was only a group of lads of 13 or 14 playing, he remembers that Ferguson was there, running his eye over the potential talent on view. At the end of the trial, just three of them were asked back – Savage among them, despite the fact that he had turned up wearing an Ian Rush shirt and, by his own account, had had 'a bit of a shocker'. It was yet another example of his fashion sense proving less than popular with those around him. On 21 November, he signed associate schoolboy terms, with a two-year apprenticeship to follow after he reached 16.

During term time, Savage continued to play in Wrexham, although now for Brickfield Rangers after Bradley had folded. This club, based at Court Road, had been founded in 1976 by a group of local parents. He would also get occasional games for United's 'B' team on Saturday mornings and joined one of Wrexham's top amateur clubs, Lex, who had been founded by a group of solicitors in the 1960s (*lex* being Latin for law). At the time, under manager Ross Sankey, the club was going through a particularly successful period. No wonder Savage's schoolwork suffered, with so much football to distract him. During the holidays, he would return to Manchester to train with United, often with the first-year apprentices.

Just as Gary Neville had been motivated by his father's

words to make the most of his opportunities at United, so was Savage. The day he signed for United as a full-time apprentice in July 1991, his father gave him a letter; the message in it was 'Hard work supplies its own reward.' It was a lesson he took to heart. As Ferguson said of him in those days: 'He had fantastic stamina; he'd run his socks off every game. He had a marvellous attitude, and that's never left the boy.' Ferguson also echoed Colin Savage's words with his own mantra: 'Practice makes players.'

The Welshman's Duracell-style performances didn't always meet with immediate approval, however, from Harrison. Simon Davies recalls one game where the manager came in at half time and told Savage to stop running around like a 'headless chicken', as there was no way he would ever keep it up for the full 90 minutes. But in the second half, Savage kept up his relentless work-rate until the end. The occasion sticks in Davies's memory because, after the game, he remembers that Harrison issued a rare apology – Savage had proved him wrong.

In a squad packed with naturally talented players, Savage and Neville knew they would have to keep working hard to have a chance – and no one would ever accuse them of shirking. Neville recalls that when he decided he could be pushing himself slightly harder in an early training session, Savage was one of a very small group (David Beckham and Chris Casper were the others) who also decided to go the extra yard. Before long, they were all doing it. As any follower of football knows, a great team needs this sort of hard-working character to succeed. Savage showed the same commitment when he played for the 'A' team, but his tally of just three goals in

15 appearances in the Lancashire League wasn't quite as prolific as would be required of a forward when he moved up a level.

Savage's regular strike partner throughout most of the cup run was Colin McKee. The forward was born in Glasgow on 22 August 1973, which made him the oldest member of the squad. He had come to United in 1989 after a club scout saw him in action for Scotland Schoolboys. He also played for Wolves Boys' Club in Carmyle, East Glasgow. The club left nothing to chance when it came to making sure they got his signature, as Ferguson came up to see him in person. 'If he turns up at your door, you don't say no,' comments lifelong United fan McKee. 'It was a dream come true.'

Like Savage, McKee could not be faulted for effort, and played much of the season for the Reserve team, making more appearances for them in the league (20) than he did for the 'A' team (11). Encouragingly from his viewpoint, his strike rate against the adults in the Pontin's League was very impressive, scoring 11 goals in all. As the step up to adult football occasionally caught out those who had been used to playing within their age groups, this was good news for him.

Both Savage and McKee were ready for action against Spurs as the whistle went for the kick-off, hoping they would be the ones to score the vital goal that would put their team through to the final. But neither of them could claim the credit when the first goal was scored, though Savage gave the assist – indeed, the scorer wasn't anyone wearing a red shirt. As David Meek reported in the *Manchester Evening News*: 'The 7,633 crowd could hardly believe their eyes as the fancied Londoners stumbled from one disaster to another.'

The match was only seven minutes old when a cross from Savage on the left wing was put into his own goal by Tottenham full-back Kevin Jordan. Four minutes later, Giggs made it 2–0. Cutting in from the left, he somehow managed to keep hold of the ball, despite seeming to lose control twice, but showing the balance and tenacity that would mark out his career, he kept going and shot home from a very tight angle. It was a stunning goal.

Giggs was on hand to take advantage of more defensive confusion after 23 minutes. A misplaced back-pass from Paul Mahorn left the goalkeeper stranded and all the Welshman had to do was tap it over the unguarded line. With the score at 3–0, it didn't seem as if things could get much worse for Spurs. But on 39 minutes they did when Nick Barmby, one of their star players, got himself sent off for dissent. Barmby had disputed a decision given against him by the linesman and such was his protest that referee Vic Callow showed him the red card. After a shambolic first-half display, the Spurs players were relieved to get into the dressing room to take stock.

It was an uncharacteristic lapse from Barmby. Born and raised in Hull, he was a few days past his 18th birthday at the time. He had begun his career playing for Springhead in the Hull Boys' Sunday Football League and for National Tigers. Clearly a terrific prospect for the future, he was also training with Hull City. At 14, he left Kelvin Hall High School to go to the FA Centre of Excellence at Lilleshall, and a glittering career beckoned for him, as by this stage he was already an England regular at junior level. After that, he signed as an apprentice for Spurs in the summer of 1990 and continued to make good progress at the club. Within another six months of this game, he made his league debut for Spurs (at the same time as fellow youth-teamer Kevin Watson), lining up alongside future England team-mates Teddy Sheringham and Darren Anderton. It was the start of a long and successful career that he brought to an end in January 2012 when he took over as permanent manager of Hull City. Twenty years on from this low point in his career, he had the chance to cheer on United's Youth Cup side, because his son Jack played a crucial part in their campaign, and by mid-March 2012 they had reached the semi-final stage, where they took on Chelsea.

Barmby wasn't the only one from the Spurs side to go on to have a distinguished career. Sol Campbell, Darren Caskey and Andy Turner were all in the line-up that performed so poorly, as well as Watson. Campbell in fact played against United as a striker, and when he made his debut for the Spurs senior side the following season he scored. Another graduate of Lilleshall, he stayed at Spurs until his controversial move across North London to Arsenal in 2001. The fact that he helped the Gunners to win the Double in his first season there may have made the move a logical one, but it certainly didn't make it any more popular with the Spurs fans. He was still at the club during the 2003–04 'Invincibles' campaign, picking up a second league title. Eventually, the England central defender moved on to Portsmouth in 2006, winning the FA Cup two years later. When he played for Newcastle in the 2010–11 season, he joined Giggs as the only two players to have appeared in each Premier League season since its start in 1992 – a record the Welshman took exclusively in 2011–12.

Although Caskey played more than 350 league games, only 32 of them were in the Premier League (for Spurs), and most of the rest were at lower levels for Reading (who signed him for £700,000) and Notts County. Like Barmby and Campbell, he was a graduate of the FA's School of Excellence. Given that he went on to captain the successful England Under-18 side in the 1993 European Championships, where he played alongside Neville, Chris Casper, Campbell and Paul Scholes in the final, and even scored the goal that won the tournament for his country, it was perhaps unsurprising that so much was expected of him.

Turner's career got off to a spectacular start when, on 5 September 1992, he set a Premier League record as the youngest goalscorer, at 17 years and 166 days (it was a half-volley from the edge of the area). However, he was loaned out to four different clubs by Spurs before eventually deciding to move on in 1996. It was the last he saw of the top level, and three substitute appearances for Northampton in 2003 were the last of his 124-game league career. His final glimpse of fame came as coach of Chasetown, appropriately enough in the third round of the FA Cup in 2008, when the Southern League side took on Cardiff City, losing 3–1.

While Hackney-born Kevin Watson had the briefest Tottenham career, making just five league appearances for them before leaving in 1996, the midfielder ended up playing more than 400 league games for various clubs, with his longest spells at Rotherham and Colchester United. He finished his career at Luton Town, moving into coaching while there, and has now become one of Sky Sports' pitch-side reporters.

Although United had been helped by the surprisingly poor form of Spurs, given the strength of their team, the fact was they had been playing very well themselves. According to the match report, they 'produced some fast-flowing football with Simon Davies outstanding in midfield, Giggs always a threat, several nice touches from Ben Thornley and some biting tackles from George Switzer'.

In the second half, if anything United were guilty of lapsing into old habits and easing off. Watson and Lee Hughes both forced good saves from Reds keeper Pilkington, and the visitors even had a goal (correctly) disallowed. It seemed like it was job done, but Harrison made sure that no complacency crept into the minds of his young side ahead of the second leg at White Hart Lane two and a half weeks later. He commented: 'We have a good lead but we have no intention of playing defensively. It would be a disservice to our lads to ask them to go for safety first. It's no way to bring up youngsters and I don't think they would know how anyway.'

United fans would hear echoes of those comments many times in the future, as the adventurous style of the apprentices was carried forward into the senior side. The second leg was a game when Harrison was forced to make some changes, too. Giggs was left out of the side so he could be kept fresh for the first team's trip to Queens Park Rangers that weekend. The senior side were trailing Leeds United by two points in the title race, but had two games in hand, so that game had absolute priority. In his place came Beckham, making his first start of the Youth Cup campaign against the club that had hoped to sign him as a boy. It was all change on the bench as well, with Joe Roberts and Lennie Taylor getting their chance.

As they always did during the Youth Cup run, United travelled down to the game in style. Ferguson insisted that their preparation should be the same as the first team's, which also meant they had to turn up in blazers looking every inch the professional footballer. It was important to the players that they did this, because it reinforced the importance of the trophy to United and put across the message that this was the nearest thing to being in the senior XI. Pilkington remembers this as a game he was particularly looking forward to, as many of his family lived in the Luton area, so it was an opportunity for them to see him in a really high-profile game.

Without Giggs, it was once again a chance for Thornley to shine. In the 16th minute, he went on yet another mazy run and delivered the perfect cross for Nicky Butt to fire home. Less than a minute later, the aggregate score was 5–0 when Thornley scored with a well-placed header. United continued to make light of the tricky conditions, dominated the rest of the first half and could have scored more, but were denied by some last-ditch defending and excellent goalkeeping.

After the break, with the result sealed, the Reds dropped their level of intensity slightly and allowed Spurs to see more of the ball. Harrison gave the fans a chance to see Taylor (on for Thornley) and Roberts (who replaced Savage) for their first appearances in the cup. Pilkington in goal also had the opportunity to show what he could do, making a series of fine saves before he was finally beaten in the 88th minute by an Andy Turner shot from just outside the box. It didn't matter, though. United had won 2–1 on the night and 5–1 on aggregate. They were back in the final.

For Taylor, just as for fellow defender Mark Gordon, who had played in the first two rounds, this game was a brief glimpse of what might have been. Both of them were released by United at the end of the season when their two-year apprenticeship came to a close. Taylor and Salford-born Gordon (known as 'Sheepy' because of his curly blond hair) were two of those players who were overshadowed by the impact made by the first-year apprentices.

Lennie Taylor was born in Aston, Birmingham, on 29 August 1974, but moved across the city to Acocks Green when he was about six years old. He went to Severne Primary School and then to Ninestiles Secondary School. His footballing journey began when some friends persuaded him to come along to a local community centre to play, and he was then invited to join North Warwickshire. After a spell at Chelmsley Wood, he began to play for a side known as the Three Cs, and it was here that he started being asked to come for trials at various clubs and began to train at Port Vale once a week.

While Taylor was playing for the Valiants one day, Ferguson (having been tipped off by a local scout) came to watch him in action and afterwards asked if he wanted to come to United. Taylor didn't say yes at once, as he felt a certain loyalty to Port Vale, but the Reds boss is not an easy man to turn down – especially if you are just 15. He went up to the Cliff to play in a trial match, lining up alongside a bunch of strangers (though he does remember that O'Kane also played with him in central defence that day), and did well enough to be offered an apprenticeship.

He signed apprentice forms in July 1990 and recalls that he

Strange as it may seem, there was a time when the crowds did not flock to see Ryan Giggs and David Beckham in action. But the signs were already there for all to see. (ABOVE) Giggs puts in one of his first crosses from the left wing. Many thousands more would follow in years to come. (BELOW) Beckham lines up a free kick from just outside the box. Goalkeepers would soon know what to expect – but doing anything about it was a different matter.

Nicky Butt powers through the midfield against Blackburn Rovers.

© *Manchester United*

Keith Gillespie was an absolute flying machine when he came to United from Northern Ireland, leading many to compare him with George Best.

© *Manchester United*

Striker Robbie Savage hurdles the challenge as United take on Liverpool. In the end, the young Welshman had to look elsewhere to develop his career.

© *Manchester United*

Scenes from the Cliff.

While the action goes on in the foreground, Eric Harrison's office window can be seen in the top right of the picture. Nothing escaped him from his vantage point.
© Manchester United

On a chilly day, some of the Class of 92 take what shelter they can in the dugout by the main building at the Cliff. L–R they are: Gary Neville, Chris Casper, Raphael Burke, John O'Kane, Nicky Butt and Robbie Savage.
© Manchester United

As word got out about the Class of 92, more and more people would come to the Cliff to see the boys in action.
© Manchester United

Kevin Pilkington, Gary Neville, George Switzer, Robbie Savage, Simon Davies and Ben Thornley pose for the cameras ahead of the 1992 Youth Cup final. © *Mirrorpix*

George Switzer charges into the Palace box at Old Trafford during the Youth Cup final on 15 May 1992.
© *Manchester United*

A jubilant United side celebrate winning the Youth Cup for the first time in 28 years after beating Crystal Palace 6–3 on aggregate. Only Colin McKee (front, right) seems to be taking it all calmly.
© *Manchester United*

Chris Casper shoots for goal during United's 5–0 victory over York City in their 1993 FA Youth Cup run. © *Mirrorpix*

Ben Thornley begins the long road to recovery after picking up the horrific injury in April 1994 that set back his career. The thumbs are up because he has been told that he will be picking up the Pontin's League trophy as Reserve team captain. © *Mirrorpix*

Colin McKee in action during his one and only first-team appearance for United, on 8 May 1994. © *Mirrorpix*

Paul Scholes celebrates with David Beckham after scoring the first of more than 150 United goals on his debut against Port Vale in the Coca-Cola Cup, 21 September 1994.
© *Action Images*

Simon Davies takes on a familiar foe, making his Premier League debut for United, as the Reds beat Crystal Palace 3–0 on 19 November 1994. © *Getty Images*

Kevin Pilkington also made his debut that day, coming on for Peter Schmeichel.
© *Action Images*

John O'Kane, one of
United's 'kids', in action
against Aston Villa in the
first game of the 1995–96
Premier League season.
© *Action Images*

One of the most
memorable goals of
all time: Ryan Giggs
blasts home past David
Seaman to clinch the FA
Cup semi-final replay
in 1999 and set up the
Treble, with the Class of
92 at the heart of it all.
© *Manchester United*

Captain Gary Neville leads the celebrations as United win the 2009 Premier League title. Between them, the Class of 92 had won 48 league titles by 2011. © *Manchester United*

David Beckham, Phil Neville and Nicky Butt applaud Gary Neville after his testimonial match on 24 May 2011, a game that saw many of the Class of 92 in action together once again. © *Manchester United*

Ryan Giggs and Paul Scholes are joined by one of the new generation of youth team graduates, Danny Welbeck, as they celebrate the Welshman's last-minute winner at Norwich City on 26 February 2012. © *Manchester United*

was used in various positions across the back line, but competition for places in the side was always fierce, 'a real dogfight', he says. While Taylor believes that, in one sense, it could have been any of them that made the real breakthrough, he recognises that Neville 'put his heart and soul in it and he deserves' all that he has achieved. He is impatient with any who criticise the most successful members of the Class of 92 for the rewards they have earned: 'They weren't there; they don't know what they went through.'

The Youth Cup final meant the end of Taylor's apprenticeship, and unfortunately for him there was no professional contract at the end of it. He went back to Port Vale and then to Walsall, who offered him another year on YTS terms, but he decided to take a step back and signed for Solihull Borough instead. He played for them for a few years before moving on to Highgate United, before eventually calling it a day. He's had various careers since football stopped paying his wages, and is now working for a property refurbishment business that takes him all over the country.

Joe Roberts at least had the consolation that he would have another year as an apprentice. Born in Crewe on 12 September 1974, Roberts had grown up in Cheshire not far from Simon Davies. He was educated at Verdin High School in Winsford, and was soon playing football for Cheshire, as well as for his school and for local club Wharton Juniors. He was a prolific goalscorer, and many clubs were keen to get him to commit to them. But Roberts's father advised caution and suggested he try out with several of them before making his decision at 14, when it would be time to sign schoolboy forms. As a result, he trained with Crewe,

Manchester City and many others, with his father having to drive him all over the region. As we have seen with many of the Class of 92, family support was a vital factor in helping him to progress.

It was when Roberts began to play for Knutsford club Allastock Lions that his talent really began to be noticed. The Lions were such a strong side that they played in the Greater Manchester competitions, rather than in Cheshire, and among their stars was Garry Flitcroft (later of Manchester City and Blackburn Rovers), who was two years older than Roberts. Their main rivals were none other than Boundary Park, and Roberts remembers early contests against Butt and Scholes when the two sides could often expect to meet each other in the finals of various competitions. The man who spotted him for United was Harry McShane, who had won the league title with the Reds in 1951–52 and who would also later discover Wes Brown.

At 14, Roberts decided that United was the club for him, and he began to train there every Monday and Thursday night, under the benevolent encouragement of Brian Kidd. Occasionally, Ferguson's assistant manager Archie Knox would take charge of the sessions, but many of the players found his Scottish accent hard to understand (though presumably McKee could help out on that). He also remembers his excitement when the boys went over to Switzerland for football tournaments during the school holidays.

When he reached 16, Roberts was given an apprentice contract and settled into the life easily. As Davies lived in nearby Middlewich, the older apprentice would give him a lift into the Cliff every day until Roberts was able to drive himself, at which stage they would alternate who would take their cars. Roberts recalled that his car was a rather aged Austin Montego that had previously belonged to his parents. The suspension had gone, so when he was giving some of his team-mates a lift from the Cliff to their training ground at Littleton Road, every bump was magnified and those in the back seats were constantly banging their heads on the roof. The life of a £29.50-a-week apprentice was not a glamorous one.

Although Roberts played only a small part in United's FA Youth Cup run, he was the leading scorer in the 'B' team that season, notching an impressive 14 goals in 20 games in the league. He remembers his two years as an apprentice as a period when the sides he was a part of were so strong: 'We used to batter teams. I can hardly remember us losing,' he says.

That Gordon, Roberts and Taylor, along with Burke and Switzer, should fall by the wayside is far from unusual. It is one of the sad things about junior football that so many players will not make it at any level with a senior club. In fact, to have just four out of the 17 players used in the Youth Cup run drop out of the game without making a single senior appearance is a remarkable hit rate, and was a superb credit to the work of United's scouting network. The Class of 92 were truly special. Now, as they looked forward to the final against Crystal Palace, they had to go out and prove it.

7

A Trip to the Palace

'They were so good, I couldn't get near it.'

Sean Daly

Final, First Leg: Tuesday 14 April 1992, Selhurst Park
Attendance: 7,825
Crystal Palace 1 Manchester United 3
Team: Pilkington; O'Kane, Neville, Casper, Switzer; Beckham, Butt, Davies, Thornley; McKee, Savage (Roberts).
Sub not used: Taylor.
Goals: Butt (17, 90), Beckham (28)

Once they had won through, 'Fergie's Fledglings' had just under three weeks to wait until the first leg of the FA Youth Cup final took place. Their opponents were the Southeast London outfit Crystal Palace, who had begun their cup run by beating local rivals Charlton Athletic 2–0. Next up, Palace crossed London to play Chelsea, and again emerged as 2–0 winners. Crewe Alexandra's famous Academy side were next to succumb, again by 2–0, as they struck a blank against the Eagles. In the quarter-finals, it was a third London side and a fourth successive scoreline of 2–0 for Crystal Palace, as they beat Matt Holland and West Ham to reach the semi-final. Almost inevitably, Palace found themselves up against yet another London side – Wimbledon – as they won through to the final 5–4 on aggregate.

With some impressive wins under their belt, and a defence that had not conceded a goal until the semi-final stage, there was no doubt that Crystal Palace presented a serious challenge to United's young team. Managed and coached by Stuart Scott and assisted by Dave Garland (who had previously been at amateur outfit Whyteleafe), they had had an excellent season, and would finish it by winning the South East Counties Division Two. Scott was the older of the two, and his tactics were usually based on the long ball, taking advantage of the physical presence of his side. A believer in firm discipline, some of the players recall they were anxious not to make a mistake in front of him. Garland, on the other hand, was seen by many of the players as being more approachable and would happily laugh and joke with them. The blend of personalities was not an unusual one in many clubs.

As usual, the Reds travelled down to London in style and comfort, but when they got there they found the weather was appalling and the pitch at Selhurst Park was heavily water-logged. Because of this, the decision as to whether it was playable wasn't taken until about an hour before kick-off.

Fortunately, the rain eased off just before the start, which ensured the game could go ahead without any problems. In the Palace changing rooms, pacey striker Grant Watts remembers how his team-mates looked through the match programme and noted how many of the United side's biographies included their junior international credentials. Palace had almost no one like that in their team. However, they were a big and powerful side, and it was those assets that had seen them through this far, often against other teams with plenty of internationals. Despite all this, they got a big lift when they noted that one name was missing from United's team-sheet, the one player they knew all about: Ryan Giggs.

The Reds fielded an unchanged side from the second leg of the semi-final, with Joe Roberts and Lennie Taylor keeping their places on the bench. In the tricky conditions, it was United who settled first and, as they had done in every round to date, got off to a great start. The first goal came when George Switzer sent Ben Thornley on a run down the left flank. His cross was met first time by Nicky Butt, who powered it past Palace keeper Jimmy Glass to give the Reds a vital early lead.

It wasn't long before United had doubled their advantage. Thornley was again involved, intercepting a back pass from Palace defender Andrew McPherson and setting up David Beckham to score after 28 minutes with a stunning left-foot volley from 25 yards. Glass recalls: 'I've only played against Beckham twice – and both times he beat me from outside the box.' (The other time was in a testimonial for Mel Machin between United and Bournemouth when Beckham nutmegged a midfielder and then unleashed an unstoppable shot from 30 yards out.) Forward Niall Thompson also remembers the future England captain from that game, but in a slightly different way. The midfielder tackled Thompson from behind, so he leaped up and grabbed him by the throat – even then, Thompson recalls, Beckham had 'bite' as well as all the skills. United were not going to be physically intimidated by the bigger side.

With a two-goal cushion to take back to Old Trafford, everything looked comfortable for the Reds. As Watts recalls, he found it hard to put pressure on Gary Neville and Chris Casper in the centre of United's defence. Fellow striker Thompson remembers Neville as a 'hard, fast and intelligent defender'. In those days, defenders could still pass back to the keeper and he was allowed to pick up the ball, so Neville and Casper took advantage of this rule to slow down the game and take the sting out of Palace's attack. Despite this, the Eagles kept going and eventually pulled back a goal through substitute Stuart McCall (on for Thompson) with just five minutes remaining. It was the goal their second-half response had probably merited, but it wasn't the last significant action of the game.

Sensing they might score an equaliser, Palace piled forward again. Centre-half Casper recalls what happened next: 'Pilkington made a great save. As he's turned round, the ball's going in, and he's cleared it with his legs and anything could have happened.' Having been spared, the Reds went straight down the other end, Beckham crossed from the right and Butt was there to finish ('He was offside,' claims Glass), ensuring the game ended 3–1 to United. The Reds had surely done enough to make the tie secure, but manager Eric

Harrison warned after the match: 'We won 3–1 on their ground and now we have to make sure they don't repeat that scoreline at Old Trafford.'

Casper also remembers that it was a very challenging evening, as the Palace side came up with a tactic that gave him and Neville plenty of trouble. Goalkeeper Glass 'could boom it a mile. It was a wicked night and he was kicking it right to the edge of our box, and they were a strong, physical side. So that was a real tough night.'

Once again, Thornley had been one of the most influential players, especially in the absence of Giggs, who had been left out of the squad ahead of the senior side's games on the following Thursday and Saturday. However, it was Butt who had had the most decisive impact of all, scoring twice to take his tally in the competition to three so far. Watts remembers that it was these two who stood out most that night: Thornley was 'very lively' while Butt just kept on 'bombing forward'.

Nicky Butt was born in the solidly working-class Gorton area, east of the centre of Manchester, on 21 January 1975. As with Paul Scholes, it was a tough background in which to grow up – West Gorton is used by the makers of *Shameless* as a location for some of the outdoor scenes in the television series. He attended Abbey Hey Primary School and then the Wright Robinson College close to Abbey Hey Lane in Gorton. By the time he was 13, he was playing for Manchester Boys, and recalls coming up against Scholes, who was in action for Rochdale Boys, and also against Gary Neville, at Bury. Of the latter, who was a midfielder at the time, he says: 'He was a very organised lad; he was very mature for his age – always sorting out other people on the pitch.'

Butt soon joined Boundary Park in Oldham, the junior football club that was founded in 1978 and has since gone on to produce more than 100 professional footballers – an extraordinary achievement. Among those who had gone before him were David Platt, United hero Mark Robins and Trevor Sinclair. Butt made an immediate impact. Their former manager Mikey Walsh remembers: 'I had two big centre-backs; they got into a bit of a scramble and they were rolling around on the floor, and as they were getting up the pair of them, Nicky just picked them up and he went bang. And when I saw that, I thought: "Yes, you'll do for me, no problem."'

When the club reached a local cup final in April 1991, their side featured not just Butt, but also Scholes and both Neville brothers. Phil Neville remembers what it was like: 'Whereas Sunday league teams used to just turn up on Sundays, Boundary Park ran it very professionally – you had training twice a week, they had tracksuits and they made sure everything was run like a professional team, really. That's probably why it attracted a lot of the best young players.' Even so, it was extraordinary that four future internationals, who would earn 249 England caps between them, should line up in the same boys' side. Not surprisingly, they won.

Butt began his United career when he came to Littleton Road in Salford on trial at the age of 13, after the club wrote to him at school inviting him to come along. There were, he recalls, about 500 there that day, all hoping to do something that would get them noticed. Butt was one of those whose talent shone out, and it was complemented by his fearless and uncompromising approach to the game. Robbie Savage describes him in those days as a 'hardcore Manc', definitely not someone to mess around with. Keith Gillespie was one who found out the hard way the accuracy of that judgement. He had a habit at the time of nudging people, only gently, but it was something that could irritate some, especially when the Irishman persisted in doing it. Butt warned him not to do it to him, but Gillespie ignored the warning and gave him a little nudge one day in the shower – and received a punch on the nose for his pains.

On the pitch, he carried the same aura about him as someone who could handle any challenge that came his way. Switzer comments: 'I always said that if one of us were going to make it – apart from Ryan – it's got to be Butty. He was just brilliant.' Clips of the youth team in action during that campaign show him as someone who was utterly fearless in the tackle, often flying into some perfectly timed fifty-fifty challenges that none but the bravest would stand up to. Davies explains just how important this was: Butt 'could change a game with a tackle', especially against those sides who tried to physically intimidate the Reds. He was living proof that United could mix it with anyone.

He was also, in those days, a fairly prolific goalscorer from midfield and was strong in the air as well. He remembers this time of his life with great happiness, playing for the Youth Cup side and for the 'A' team, often attracting the first-teamers to watch them in action. No wonder Phil Neville adds, 'Everyone was saying he was the next Bryan Robson: he was scoring goals.' For Harrison, Butt was just his sort of player, someone who would give everything to the cause: 'He was a man when he was sixteen was Nicky Butt.'

Partnering Butt in the centre of midfield throughout the competition was Simon Davies. Along with Switzer and Colin McKee, he was one of just three second-year apprentices to make the team for this game. Born in Middlewich, Cheshire, on 23 April 1974, he had been on Manchester City's books since the age of nine. He'd joined a club called the Lostock Lions in Northwich, which was run by someone who was also a City scout, and he had recommended Davies to the club. He went to City for training every Thursday night and had trials there during the school holidays.

As Davies approached his 14th birthday, City made moves to formalise the arrangement, offering him a deal based on two years as a schoolboy and then two years as an apprentice. It was then that fate took a turn. A week before his birthday, he was in action in Salford against Salford Boys and, although his side lost 2–1, he played well and scored a goal. Watching on was a United scout, who approached his father to ask if Davies would be interested in coming to United for trials. His father explained the situation, and how his son was due to sign for City in a week's time. As a United fan, he hoped the club might step in for his son. They didn't let him down.

United didn't waste any time; Ferguson had energised the scouting department and they knew they were expected to sign up any promising talent – especially if that talent was thinking of going to Maine Road. Explaining to Ferguson why someone ended up wearing a blue shirt rather than a red one was a conversation they preferred not to have. So a game was arranged for the Monday evening, and Davies again performed well, impressing the club. The next day, Ferguson and Joe Brown, now youth development officer, turned up at his house and signed Davies. He recalls how it happened: 'I think my mum got the posh cups out [when Ferguson called round] and my sister actually said: "Mum, why have we got the cups out?" "Well, we've got a guest." Because usually we got all the ones with the chipped cups.' So within three days, he had gone from a City schoolboy prospect to becoming a United player – all thanks to two excellent performances and some very smart crockery.

Now, almost four years to the day since that moment when he'd first impressed United, Davies was still impressing all the right people at the club – and making it very hard for Crystal Palace to get back into the game for the second leg, which would take place at Old Trafford. But what of the Palace side? How did their stories compare with those of the United players in reaching this stage? And how did their careers proceed afterwards? The comparison helps to highlight why it is that the Class of 92 stand out as the pinnacle of what can be achieved by a youth team, and how different the outcomes usually are.

Certainly, for anyone who thought life was tough for United's apprentices, with the various initiation rites they had to endure, the picture that emerges from Palace is that things were if anything more challenging there 20 years ago. Forward Niall Thompson recalls how one of their number had a reputation for being a little bit too cocky, so they decided to put him in his place. One day, this player was last to emerge from the showers after training, and when he came out the rest of the apprentices threw a towel over him and took it in turns to punch him. When they'd finished, he was bleeding and bruised, but he responded by saying 'Is that it?' Within a few weeks, however, he had quit the club.

Without a doubt the most successful player to emerge from the youth ranks of the Eagles was George Ndah. The Camberwell-born midfielder had begun his career at local club Dulwich Hamlet, where he was spotted by Palace, who are based a couple of miles down the road from Hamlet's Champion Hill ground, and signed up. He was quickly drafted into the youth side and performed well. In 1992–93, Palace manager and ex-United star Steve Coppell, having given him a taste of senior action in the Coca-Cola Cup, had no qualms about throwing him into a Premier League debut at Anfield against Liverpool. It was the first of 13 appearances that campaign, concluding with another run-out at Old Trafford. Along with striker Watts, he was the only member of the Youth Cup final side to make a league appearance that season. One year after the final, there wasn't a huge difference between the two sides in terms of how their careers had progressed at the senior level.

Ndah never really established himself as a regular starter at the club, and on 21 November 1997 he was transferred to Swindon Town for £500,000, where Steve McMahon was the manager. By now, he was playing more usually as a forward and in 1998–99 had his most prolific season, scoring 12 goals for the Robins. His form was noted by Colin Lee at Wolverhampton Wanderers, and on 21 October 1999 the club signed him for £1 million. Sadly, just a few weeks later, he broke his leg in his third game for his new team. For the rest of his career, injuries would plague him. His commitment to the club, and his battles to regain full fitness, helped make him a popular figure among the Black Country fans. Towards the end of 2005–06, he called time on his playing career, having made 248 league appearances in total (just 25 of them in the top flight), and scoring 39 goals. Had it not been for his injuries, those figures could have been much higher. As we will see, Ndah was not the only player in action during the final whose career was to be severely blighted by injury problems.

Goalkeeper Jimmy Glass was another from the Palace side who had a decent professional career. Born in Epsom on 1 August 1973, he was a comparative veteran for the Youth Cup, as this was his third year in the competition, and he was (along with Giggs, who played in the second leg) the only one on either side who was already a full professional, then earning about £200 a week. He says he didn't take his football particularly seriously until he had trials with Chelsea at the age of 14. After a few weeks, they let him go, but Palace scout Vic Pennington suggested he tried out for them. He had more luck there, and at 16 was taken on as an apprentice – just like the United players, he started on £29.50 per week plus expenses.

Unfortunately, as was the case with United's keeper Kevin Pilkington (who had Peter Schmeichel to compete with), making the breakthrough to the first team was almost impossible. The Palace goalie at the time was Nigel Martyn, who was then vying with David Seaman for the England keeper's jersey, and never seemed to miss a match – in those days there was much less squad rotation, even when it came to the Coca-Cola Cup, for example. So, on 10 February 1995,

Glass was loaned out to Portsmouth to provide back-up to the experienced Alan Knight and finally made his first-team debut eight days later. Just over a year after that, he was given a free transfer to Bournemouth, where he got a regular run in the side, playing every game of the 1997–98 season.

That summer, however, he was given a free transfer to Swindon, where he again linked up with Ndah, but when he couldn't displace Frank Talia, he was loaned out to Carlisle United, where Michael Knighton was both chairman and manager, on 22 April 1999. And it was here that he became a local hero. In the final match of the season, the Cumbrian side were drawing 1–1 with Plymouth Argyle, a result that would have meant relegation from the Football League. With four minutes of injury time nearly over, and with the crowd of 7,599 (the biggest of the season) roaring them on, Carlisle's 71 years in the Football League looked to be coming to an end. They earned a corner and Glass was urged to come forward. The corner was headed goalwards and cleared off the line – but who should be there to volley home from the edge of the six-yard box but Glass. Before he'd moved a few yards to begin his celebrations he was submerged under a pile of fans who had surged on to the pitch. 'That moment was the best point in my life – being carried off the football pitch by seven and a half thousand happy, screaming fans.'

It was a moment of pure football fantasy, straight out of the pages of *Roy of the Rovers* – the goalkeeper who scored the vital winning goal with the last kick of the game. But the reality was that Glass would play very few more games in the Football League. Indeed, it was ironic that while he was saving Carlisle with a last-minute goal from a corner, his opponents from seven years earlier were just about to complete their famous Treble – also thanks to a last-minute winner from a corner.

Within a couple of years, he decided to call time on his career, and it was only in the autumn of 2011 that he renewed his involvement in the game, inspired by the enthusiasm of his children for football, and he is currently helping Poole Town as a goalkeeping coach.

But Glass's story doesn't end with the drama of the Carlisle goal, for in January 2011 he was back in the news. Or, more precisely, his wife Louise was. At that stage he was living quietly in Dorset, running a taxi firm, when Richard Keys made the notorious comments to Jamie Redknapp about her that led to Keys's departure from Sky Sports. Understandably, he would much rather dwell on his own moment of fame than Keys's moment of infamy.

Glass wasn't the only member of the Crystal Palace youth team to get caught up in a major news story many years later. Russell Edwards was another one who found himself at the centre of a media storm. The Beckenham-born defender never managed a first-team game for the Eagles, but in 1993–94 moved across London to join Barnet, making his league debut in March 1994. However, by the age of 20, his league career was over. He played for a variety of non-league sides, including Ndah's old club Dulwich Hamlet (where former Palace youth coach Garland also managed) and Welling United.

While Edwards was at Chelmsford City he met Paul Nicholls, who would later go on to become John Terry's agent. When Edwards subsequently set up a marketing firm called Riviera Entertainment, they sent out an email in November 2009 offering the then England captain as a potential 'high-profile brand ambassador', which set off a media outcry.

Despite being such a strong team at youth level, only a few of the Palace players made even one league appearance – a dramatic contrast to their United opponents. Skipper Mark Holman was loaned to Welling in March 1993 and released by Palace in 1994. In 2012, he was at Meifod FC, a struggling club in the Spar Mid Wales League Two situated a few miles from Welshpool in Powys.

Team-mate Mark Hawthorne was one of the few who did play in the Football League, though he had to move away from Selhurst Park to do so. The Glasgow-born midfielder joined Torquay United in 1994–95 and made his debut for them on 25 March 1995, but was given a free transfer at the end of the 1996–97 season, after making a total of 58 league appearances, and moved to Crawley. He played for various non-league clubs after that, and in January 2012 was named manager of Horsham YMCA.

Palace's goalscorer Stuart McCall, along with full-back Scott Cutler (who now lives in New Zealand), and midfielders Andy McPherson and Simon Rollison were all gone from the club by the end of the following season and never made any first-class appearances. The same was true of Sean Daly, who had grown up in nearby Colliers Wood. He'd started his career at Wimbledon, and at 14 won a place at Lilleshall, where he roomed with Sol Campbell, United's semi-final foe. While there, Garland offered him an apprenticeship at Palace in July 1990.

A Trip to the Palace

Daly didn't play at all in the first leg, but was on the bench for the Old Trafford game and remembers watching on, with Giggs in particular catching his eye: 'I'd never seen anyone so quick on the ball.' Although usually a defender, when he came on in the second half he played in midfield, up against Butt, who was another who stood out for him. 'I think I touched the ball about twice,' he remembers. 'They were so good, I couldn't get near it.'

Despite this experience, Daly was offered a two-year professional contract in the summer, and subsequently moved on to Fulham. However, he too suffered from a badly broken leg and was released. After that, he played for a series of clubs in South London, including Croydon, Sutton United, Carshalton and Dulwich Hamlet. His final club was AFC Wimbledon, where it had all started for him, before ankle problems brought his career to a premature end. As early as his spell at Fulham, when he was undergoing rehab for his injury, he had started to plan for the future, first working as a trainer in a gym and later qualifying to become an electrician, and he is now self-employed in that business.

Of the rest, forward Grant Watts was a local lad from Croydon who got his chance in the first team on 12 December 1992 when he came on as a substitute for fellow Youth Cup star Ndah. At the time he was a prolific goalscorer, often playing right on the shoulder of the last defender, ready to use his pace to pounce (Javier Hernández is probably the most similar in style to him in United's current line-up). He began to make his mark at Selsdon Juniors, a club that had a similar local status to Boundary Park in Greater Manchester. Run by a Palace scout, many of

Selsdon's best players moved across to the Eagles (Holman and Edwards were just two of the others to take this route), which was how Watts came to join them at the age of 14.

In 1993–94, Palace had a new manager, Alan Smith, and Watts felt he didn't have the same rapport with him as he had with Coppell, so he went out on loan to Colchester, before moving to Gillingham and Sheffield United. He was gearing up for the next stage of his career when his leg was so badly broken in a game that his foot was pointing in the wrong direction. It was some three years before he was back to full fitness – and even then he had lost some of the pace that had been one of his main assets. The injury had effectively ended his career before it had even begun. Now he runs his own construction business.

Meanwhile, forward Niall Thompson didn't ever make the first team at Palace, and his registration with the club was cancelled during 1993–94. He was anything but a local boy made good, and had the most unusual route to the Youth Cup final of anyone on either side. Although he was born in Birmingham, his family had moved out to Canada when he was two. While there, he had played junior international football, and experienced big crowds when they travelled to Central America. He came to Europe aged 17 for trials at PSV Eindhoven at the time that Bobby Robson was their manager. Robson still had contacts at his former club Ipswich Town, and as they had two established Canadians on their books (Frank Yallop and Craig Forrest), he was sent there for a trial, as it was believed they would help him to settle in. The trial went well, and Thompson scored three goals in two games, but he was hugely disappointed when they decided against taking him on. Fortunately, his uncle Jim then contacted Crystal Palace to alert them to the availability of a young Canadian international. They were impressed by what they saw and took him on as a second-year apprentice.

He recovered from the disappointment of being let go by Palace and the following campaign joined Colchester United, scoring five goals in 13 games. But when he was given a free transfer, he decided to try his luck in North America (playing for various clubs in Canada and the US) and in Belgium. There were still occasional appearances in England – a spell at Brentford in 1998 and one for Wycombe Wanderers in 2000–01 – but that was it. He has now returned to the country where he grew up and is managing Surrey United in Canada.

For a team that were able to battle their way through to the final of the Youth Cup and show such promise on a consistent basis over that season, the fact that so few players went on to have long professional careers may seem surprising. In fact, it is pretty much what usually happens to even the best youth teams when they reach senior level. Looking back on it, Glass wonders if one key to the difference came from the very top.

At Palace, manager Steve Coppell was 'fantastic – the best player in training', according to Glass, even a decade after he'd had to retire from the game through knee problems. However, Thompson says the youth team saw very little of him, and that his influence on things must have gone on behind the scenes. But he moved on in the summer of 1993, resigning after the club were relegated from the Premier League. Over the next decade, the club had 11 managers before Iain Dowie was able to create a period of relative stability. In such an environment, giving young players an opportunity and a chance to learn the game and make mistakes was unlikely. It takes a brave manager to do that, and when the average period in charge for a Palace boss was about a year, it was much more difficult to take that risk. At United, however, Alex Ferguson was both willing and able to do just that.

Glass comments that Ferguson's and United's approach – building from within – was almost unique at that time. The club weren't afraid to spend big money to bring in new players, as the signing of Roy Keane a year later would show. But mostly they wanted to develop players from scratch if at all possible, teaching them the United way. It was a logic that had worked 40 years before for Matt Busby. Now it was up to the new generation to prove they could take on that mantle and finish the job when Palace came back to Old Trafford for the second leg. It was a game that could help define these youngsters, but it was also one that would have significance for the famous old stadium.

8

The Magnificent Seventh

'Still one of my proudest achievements.'

Gary Neville

Final, Second Leg: Friday 15 May 1992, Old Trafford
Attendance: 14,681
Manchester United 3 Crystal Palace 2
Team: Pilkington; O'Kane, Neville, Casper, Switzer; Beckham, Butt, Davies (Savage), Thornley (Gillespie); McKee, Giggs.
Goals: Thornley (35), Davies (50), McKee (68)

With the second leg of the final of the FA Youth Cup to be held at Old Trafford, Reds fans felt there was every chance the trophy would be coming back to its spiritual home for a record-breaking seventh time, albeit after an absence of 28 years. There was no doubt about this being an important moment in the club's history and the *Manchester Evening*

News gave the game a hefty preview that day: 'Red-Hot Kids on the Brink' was the headline.

Skipper Simon Davies was quoted as saying: 'We feel we are better than Palace and now we hope to prove it.' But for this game, he was to lose the captain's armband to the returning Ryan Giggs, who was given the chance to play in his last Youth Cup game. If successful, it would not be the Welshman's first significant piece of silverware that season, for on 12 April he had been part of the United team that beat Nottingham Forest 1–0 at Wembley to secure the Rumbelows (League) Cup. Sadly, there had been no league title to go with it. In an eight-day spell, United had played four games and gained just one point in the league and so allowed the title to slip from their grasp and into the grateful hands of Leeds United. Winning the Youth Cup would be some consolation for that disappointment.

Davies stressed that United were not overconfident and were aware of the threat posed by the Eagles: 'Palace are a physical side and they put us under a lot of pressure near the end. But we scored in the last thirty seconds to take a two-goal lead, which obviously gives us a tremendous advantage. But we won't be looking for a draw. We want to win.' Youth-team manager Eric Harrison reinforced that point: 'They wouldn't know how to play for a draw. We don't teach them that kind of football.'

It was an important game for Harrison, too – a vital achievement to add to his CV, as he acknowledged: 'Our youngsters have done well in their local competitions. The "A" team have won the Lancashire League six times out of the last nine and have been runners-up the other three seasons.

Perhaps we should have done better in the FA Youth Cup. Tonight we hope to put that right.'

There was another reason why the win was important, as Alex Ferguson commented: 'We don't like to go overboard about young players, but this lot are very exciting. With their ability and desire to play they should go far. Winning the FA Youth Cup can be significant. When Manchester United last won it in 1964 it triggered the best period in the club's post-Munich history.'

Winning the cup wasn't just about adding some silverware to the trophy cabinet; it was about creating a springboard for the club in the future. If this group of youngsters could cope with the pressure of a cup final and the growing level of expectation within the club and among the fans, who had been coming to watch them in increasing numbers, then they might just have the chance to make a breakthrough at senior level. As Harrison told the paper: 'I am very thrilled with this team. It's the best youth side I have had and the bonus is that they are mostly first-year trainees, which means they are eligible next season. It is most unusual to have such a good side from a first-year intake.'

In fact, with Giggs's selection ahead of Robbie Savage up front, there were four second-years in the team, while the other nine in the squad were first-years. That was the only change to the starting line-up, but Savage had the compensation of a place on the bench, and Keith Gillespie also returned to be the other substitute. For Palace, Niall Thompson had flown back to Canada to play for the national Under-20s side in a tournament in his home town of Vancouver, so Stuart McCall, who had come off the bench to score in the first leg, took his place. Grant Watts was struggling with an injury, so was fit enough only for the bench, and Tim Clark was moved up from defence to play in a more forward role. This gave Paul Sparrow his chance in the starting line-up.

While the presence of Giggs undoubtedly gave United a lift, and would have worried Palace, one man was less happy about it. Savage had started every game in the run-up to the second leg. He had no issues with Giggs playing, 'but instead of me?' He had been looking forward to the game as 'the pinnacle' of his first season at United, and as a popular, hard-working member of the squad this was the time he most wanted to be in the thick of it all with his friends and team-mates – not sitting on the bench. He admits he was 'devastated' to be left out. He did come on to replace Davies with 20 minutes left, and even had a chance to score when Giggs set him up, but a slight bobble meant he miscued with the goal at his mercy. When the celebrations began, he says: 'I didn't feel part of it … When you win and don't play, it's still good, but it's not the same. It was the first medal I've had – I've only had two!' To make matters worse, after the game he learned his mother had had to go to hospital, so he dashed off to see her in Wrexham.

Because of the physical threat Palace had posed United in the first leg, Harrison had spent a lot of time working on that aspect in training, as Chris Casper recalls: 'We'd been prac-tising set pieces because they were pretty strong on set pieces. So we got everything nailed down, who was going with which man.' This preparation meant they all felt ready to handle whatever might come their way, and they were eager and ready for action.

The Magnificent Seventh

The game kicked off at 7.30, and by 7.31 the Eagles had won a corner. Scott Cutler swung it in and Andy McPherson rose high to head home to bring the aggregate score back to 3–2. Casper remembers, 'All hell let loose.' At the interval, Kevin Pilkington recalls being on the receiving end of a blast from Harrison: 'Any chance of you coming out for a cross in the second half?' he demanded.

This goal could have derailed United's young side, but they calmly went about playing their football. As Davies comments, 'That was the test.' Could the players recover from this early setback? He began to get a grip on the midfield, perhaps helped by the boots he was wearing. 'I actually wore Paul Ince's boots in the final, because I cleaned his boots, along with a few other first-teamers' boots, and I asked him if I could wear his boots in the final and he let me.'

Davies played a key part in United's superb equaliser, which came in the 35th minute. It was a great move that began when left-back George Switzer passed the ball up to Nicky Butt, who knocked it back under pressure to Davies. He then lifted a perfectly weighted pass down the left wing from the halfway line to Ben Thornley. The local lad surged forward along the flank, then cut inside the box and unleashed a fierce right-foot shot into the far corner of the goal from a narrow angle.

No wonder David Beckham has commented: 'Some of the football we played, even when I look back at it now, no one could get near us. That's not being big-headed . . . To experience that at such a young age was something that I'll never forget.'

Thornley knew the importance of his strike: 'I scored the

goal that took us back to another two-goal lead again, and the relief around the team and around Eric Harrison at half time was there for all to see. I thought that one goal I'd just scored could give us the cushion to go on and win it.'

Once again, the role of Thornley was a vital one, as he proved himself to be one of the real stars of the side. David Meek wrote of him: 'The Bury-born winger and former England Schoolboy showed a great range of skills and won a standing ovation when he was substituted because of injury late in the game.'

But it was another local lad, described by the *Evening News* as 'the fans' favourite', who set up the crucial second goal. Switzer, it was said, combined a 'steely but skilful approach' in his play. His retelling of that moment may need to be taken with a small pinch of salt: 'I've done a one-two with Si[mon Davies] and made a ninety-five-yard run [he laughs] and I had a shot and it rebounded and Si scored.'

According to what the cameras showed, it happened like this. The Salford-born left-back picked up the ball just inside his own half and surged forward with it, getting almost as far as the edge of the Palace box. He played a one-two with Davies, bustled into the box, and shot from a narrow angle. Keeper Jimmy Glass made the save, but it rebounded out to Davies who blasted the ball home from eight yards.

Switzer continues: 'Everyone ran to Si and I ran off to the crowd to the Main Stand and I was just like that [pumping his fists]. Like, sod them, I made the goal!' No wonder he was such a favourite with the crowd – he played with such enthusiasm and responded so well to their urgings.

The Magnificent Seventh

With the aggregate score now 5–2, some of the energy went out of Palace's response; although they did manage to equalise on the night soon after the hour mark, the tie was as good as won. To seal it, Thornley ran inside from the left flank and passed to Giggs on the corner of the box, who crossed first time for Colin McKee to head home unopposed from eight yards out in the centre of the goal.

The score remained 3–2 on the night and 6–3 on aggregate, and Old Trafford was able to celebrate success in the Youth Cup. It was a significant night for the ground, too, for that game was the last played before the old Stretford End terracing was pulled down so that a new stand could be built in its place. In the aftermath of the Hillsborough Disaster, all major clubs had to convert their grounds to all-seater stadiums. So while events on the pitch suggested it might be the start of a new era, for those who had spent many years coming to M16 to watch their football, it was also the end of an era on the terraces. No longer would fans be able to stand to watch United in action – seating was the way forward.

Giggs led the team to receive the trophy, and even with some senior silverware already in his trophy cabinet at home, he knew this was a significant moment: 'At that stage of your career, it's bigger than anything. It's the biggest trophy that you can win, so the lads were delighted to win, and we deserved it because we played some great football and scored some great goals.'

Gary Neville echoes those thoughts: 'It's like the European Cup of youth football. You ask any youth-team player: all they want to do is to win the Youth Cup, and it was our dream to win the Youth Cup and we were happy we'd done it in style. We'd beaten the best teams. It gave us the confidence to go on and play football the way that we have done.' He adds that winning the Youth Cup is 'still one of my proudest achievements ... because it was such a fantastic team to be a part of.'

For Palace, their manager Steve Coppell recognised that they had been beaten by an excellent team: 'The performance of the United boys is a pointer for a very healthy future. It's clear that the conveyor belt producing young players is rolling again at Old Trafford. There is quality in the team and they have certainly struck a rich seam with the side which played against us.'

Ferguson was pleased not only by the result – especially coming after the disappointment of the league campaign – but with all the work that had been done at the club to reach this moment: 'I had to make some hard but common-sense decisions soon after I arrived with our scouting set-up. Brian Kidd at local level has been a tremendous influence with the scouting of youngsters. We saturated the Manchester area and the result is that seven of last night's team all came from the Greater Manchester or Lancashire area.'

Having won the trophy, it was time to celebrate. The cameras followed the players into their changing room, and sure enough the bubbles were flowing. But in those days the bubbles came from lemonade, not champagne. What happened next is the subject of some debate and possibly hazy memories from those who were there, which some might think would suggest that they moved on to something a little stronger at some stage of the evening. Nicky Butt remembers going to a house party near Giggs's home, but 'nothing mad'.

Giggs says they all went on to Discotheque Royale on Whitworth Street, an old stomping ground at the time. Neville believes they didn't even go out as a team. To that, Giggs responded, 'Well, Gaz probably did go home, actually. He probably had training the next day or something, the professional that he is. But a lot of the lads went out.'

For only one of the United team could it be said that this sort of success was 'in the blood'. Chris Casper was born in Burnley on 28 April 1975 and was the son of Frank, who'd had a 15-year playing career at Rotherham United and Burnley, retiring in 1976. While at the Lancashire club, he had helped them regain top-flight status for the last time until 2009–10. After retiring, Frank had moved into coaching, initially at youth level but eventually becoming manager of Burnley from 1989 to October 1991. Chris Casper was educated at St Theodore's School in Burnley, which had an excellent local reputation for its sporting facilities. As well as playing for the school, he also joined Barrowford Celtic.

Given Casper's family background, it was perhaps not surprising that Ferguson should say of him: 'Chris Casper was probably the best professional of them all, because he came from a football background. His whole life was dedicated to playing the game, every aspect of it, through his father Frank. It was sheer professionalism.' Perhaps because of this, he was very vocal during matches; as Beckham commented, 'It was like lining up alongside a commentator.'

On hearing from MUTV that Ferguson had complimented him on his professional approach, Casper was not only flattered but tried to explain why he thought the manager had said that: he always trained hard, he was impeccably turned out, and he was a great believer that if a meeting was called for ten o'clock you should aim to be there 15 minutes early. It was unfortunate that this final comment drew only laughter from his interviewer – he had turned up 30 minutes late for the interview!

Casper also highlighted another reason why his father's role in his career was important. 'We used to talk an awful lot about football . . . I think people miss the importance of that. It's part of your learning.' He adds that while practice is certainly vital if one is to do well, 'there's talking about the game and [watching] the elite players'. He remains grateful that at no stage did his father push him into football, nor did he try to sway his decision about where to go when the scouts came calling.

Among them were United. Casper had come to their attention when he was 13, and, as is so often the case, luck played a part in it. Joe Brown was one of the most influential figures in United's scouting set-up, and as he was a former manager of Burnley, having been in charge there during 1976–77, he not only knew Frank Casper but kept a close eye on the club. He saw the young Casper in action in an Under-14 derby game against Blackburn, which even at that age was a significant fixture (the intensity of the local rivalry often surprises those who know little of that part of Lancashire). In those days, Casper was playing in midfield, and he recalls: 'I used to play in the middle of the park. I used to enjoy it, better than keeping on defending all the time – getting forward and trying to score a few goals. It was good.' Certainly he was good too, and soon he was on his way to Manchester to join the rest of the young lads there.

As well as being a Burnley fan, for obvious reasons, Casper was also a United fan, having been won over to the Reds by the 1983 FA Cup final victory over Brighton. Once he heard they were interested in him, he knew straight away it was an opportunity he could not turn down. When he arrived at Old Trafford, he realised he was joining 'the biggest club in the world, but it was also very friendly and a little bit intimidating and awe-inspiring'.

Because of his youth, Casper had not started the campaign in the centre of defence, but had been on the bench for the first two rounds. When he did make his debut, it was in the Manchester derby at the expense of John O'Kane, who was moved out to right-back, while Mark Gordon lost his place in the starting line-up entirely.

Born in Nottingham on 15 November 1974, O'Kane had started his career playing junior football locally and had been getting interest from the two clubs in his home town. However, his reputation had spread beyond the East Midlands, and he had been contacted by several other clubs, as he was a natural at the game. Then one day Nobby Stiles turned up to watch him play, and asked if he'd like to join United. O'Kane and his parents were invited to see the first team in action at Old Trafford at the start of the 1989–90 season, so he was in the crowd when Michael Knighton performed his famous ball-juggling act in front of the Stretford End. The O'Kanes were also invited round to Ferguson's house so they could hear from the manager precisely what was on offer. After that they were hardly going to turn round and say no to United.

A tall, leggy defender, O'Kane was unusual in the Class of

92 in that he was much more laid-back than the rest (one team-mate described him as 'horizontal'). He will admit that he did not have anything like the same work ethic that most of the others possessed. He wasn't above playing the odd prank on the pitch, either. Lining up alongside Casper, who he says was a bit like Alan Hansen ('very classy'), he would sometimes send him a hospital pass just to wind him up.

As a consequence of living in digs, in his early days at the club, 'Scon' (as he was nicknamed, for reasons unknown) became close friends with another of the players who had come to United from further away: David Robert Joseph Beckham. He too was on the receiving end of O'Kane's pranks in the digs they shared. 'Me and Paul Gough [another trainee] used to wind him up and move all his aftershaves and suits, because he liked them lined up perfectly.' Lennie Taylor, who was also in the same digs, adds: '[Beckham] was very particular ... He was in a class of his own as far as that went.' But life there was 'pure laughs'.

Born in Leytonstone on 2 May 1975, Beckham had been something of a child prodigy. He grew up in Chingford, and spent many happy hours playing in Chase Lane Park. His father Ted was a keen amateur footballer and the young David would often go along to watch his father in action (the roles would soon be reversed). Even at the age of seven, Beckham would be challenged to see if he could chip a ball on to the crossbar from the edge of the box, with a 50p prize every time he did it. It was the first step to becoming the wealthiest footballer on the planet.

Educated at Chase Side Primary School and Chingford

High School, Beckham joined local club Ridgeway Rovers, where the game was taken very seriously: you had to train during the week if you were to be considered for a place in the side at the weekend. As with Boundary Park in Oldham, it was a club that developed a professional attitude very early on in its players. His performances for Ridgeway got him noticed by his district side, Waltham Forest, and at county level for Essex.

Soon he was picked up by Tottenham Hotspur, the team his father supported, where he played alongside the likes of Nick Barmby and Sol Campbell, years before they lined up on opposite sides in the Youth Cup. However, for all of Spurs' famous past, his eyes were fixed on another club with a great history: he wanted to play for Manchester United. His only concern was that he had no way of knowing how they were ever going to spot him from so far away. But, at the age of 11, two things changed all that.

First of all, he entered a competition held by the Bobby Charlton Soccer School, the final of which took place on the Old Trafford pitch just before a game between United and Spurs. Beckham was one of three winners, and by far the youngest, and earned his chance to go to Barcelona to train with the club there. At the time, Terry Venables was the manager at the Nou Camp and he greeted the three winners.

His second piece of good fortune came when United scout Malcolm Fidgeon came to watch Waltham Forest in action at Redbridge. Fidgeon immediately notified the club that he had found a great prospect and Beckham was invited up to Old Trafford. They made a huge fuss of him: he was invited to be a mascot for one game, and was asked into the first-team changing room where he met the players. Ferguson made sure he personally greeted Beckham and his family. He might have been a Londoner, but he was immediately made to feel at home in Manchester.

Of course, United weren't the only ones after Beckham when it came time to sign schoolboy terms. Spurs were keen to make the arrangement with him more permanent, and the lure of the North London club – his father's team, his local side – was strong. However, when he went to talk things through, Venables (who was now in charge at White Hart Lane) didn't recognise him from when they had met at Barcelona. The contrast with United was significant and, as Beckham wrote in his memoirs: 'It always felt like you were part of a family at United.'

There was no doubt where his heart wanted him to go, but Beckham admits that there was also a hard-headed calculation involved, too. Spurs made the first offer, giving him two years on schoolboy terms, two years as an apprentice, and two years as a professional. He decided that if United matched that six-year offer, whatever the money was he would go with the Reds. He travelled up to Old Trafford with his father, and there to meet him was not only Ferguson but also scout Fidgeon and youth development officer Les Kershaw. It was his birthday, too, so the club had bought him a cake (yet again showing the meticulous attention to detail that can make all the difference). When Ferguson unveiled his offer, it was also for six years, and though the money wasn't as good in the final analysis, it was all Beckham needed to hear. He knew he wanted to be a United player, and the club wanted him.

Initially, of course, Beckham played and trained at United only during the school holidays, but he knew this was the beginning of a long road: 'The day I signed didn't feel like the day I'd made it. The hard work was just starting.' On his trips up to Manchester, he would stay in halls of residence in Salford and remembers not only the relaxed O'Kane but also Colin Murdock from Scotland and Gillespie.

Eventually, in 1991, he moved up to Manchester on a permanent basis. He didn't settle in his first digs, but after moving around eventually was sent to digs with Ann and Tom Kay, who lived near the Cliff, which made it ideal for him and O'Kane. He was one of the few who had a steady girlfriend at the time, but occasionally found that he was torn between spending time with her and hanging out with his friends. Meanwhile, his parents continued to be keen supporters of his career, and made great sacrifices to come to cheer him on. The Beckhams and the Nevilles became close friends, as they spent so many days on the touchline watching their boys in action.

It wasn't just the parents who became close. Beckham and Neville shared the same work ethic, as we have seen. The two of them would regularly go back to the Cliff for extra training, while Harrison coached the Under-16s. Already they were setting standards of dedication and professionalism that not only rubbed off on others but ensured they would both have the grounding to keep on going throughout their careers.

There was no doubt that, even then, Beckham was a bit different from the others. Because of his long association with the club, where he had sometimes been able to help out in the changing rooms as a boy, he had got to know kit man Norman Davies before he became an apprentice, and Norman ensured that the Londoner usually got the best kit. It reinforced the view of some that he was a bit of a flash Cockney. Not only that, but he was unusually tidy for a teenager (and, when he was old enough, he was the one who bought Giggs's old car).

There was no danger of Harrison giving Beckham, or anyone else, special treatment in the way the kit man did, however. As we have seen, he made sure they all learned the virtues of hard work, but on top of that he wanted to make sure his players could look after themselves on the pitch. This was vital to prepare them for the time when they would come up against adult sides, or bigger opponents such as Palace. Beckham recalls one training exercise – 'Headers' – where the midfielders and forwards were allowed to score only by heading the ball. They were put up against the team's biggest defenders and had to win the aerial battle against the likes of Casper, who was much larger than most of the rest of them. As Beckham was something of a late developer, this was a particularly tough challenge. He remembers emerging from these sessions covered in bruises. But if he would soon be taking on the likes of left-backs Stuart Pearce and Julian Dicks, it was ideal preparation for what lay ahead.

Fortunately, as his first year as an apprentice continued, he filled out and began to find the strength to match his talent. The fitness had always been there – Savage reckoned he and Beckham were the two with the most stamina in the group – but now he had the physical presence to go with it. He became an increasingly important part of the side by 1992, having been more of a peripheral figure in the first half of the season. It was one reason why he played more games that campaign for the 'B' team than for the 'A' team, achieving a notably higher strike rate at the lower level: eight goals in 15 appearances as opposed to one in 12. At the start of the season, he had often been competing with Keith Gillespie for a position wide on the right, but had usually lost out to the Ulsterman. Later on, this was rarely the case, and Gillespie often moved to a more forward, central role to accommodate him, especially when Savage was struggling with one or two injuries he had picked up.

When not toughening up his players by getting them used to the normal knocks and bruises of a match, Harrison was also building their mental strength – especially when it came to dealing with criticism, of which there was plenty. For Beckham, it was his tendency to play 'Hollywood passes' that caused the manager's ire. Even in those days, Beckham's distribution skills were excellent, and his ability to hit long passes was unmatched within the group, but when his efforts went astray Harrison did not let him get away with it. 'Well, if Hollywood passes are trying something outrageous and giving the ball away to the opposition, I did shout at him for it,' he says. While Harrison might have remained unconvinced by it all, for one of his team-mates it showed how Beckham had something special about him. Davies was impressed that Beckham kept on trying his long passes, as it showed his belief in his own ability, whatever Harrison said. Little did anyone suspect that 20 years later, Beckham would still be playing true Hollywood passes – for his LA Galaxy side.

With the season now over, Beckham and the rest of the victorious Youth Cup side could forget about impressing Harrison for a few weeks and enjoy the break. When they came back for the 1992–93 campaign, most of the team were looking not only to retain their hold on the trophy, but one or two began to think they might just start to have a chance to follow Giggs into the first team. That was very definitely the next target for the Class of 92.

9

Making the Step Up or Crashing Out

'I have never seen their like before.'

Alex Ferguson

When the FA Youth Cup-winning side returned for training after the summer break in 1992, things were very different for most of them. For a start, as second-year apprentices their pay had shot up from £29.50 per week to £39.50, while those players (such as Simon Davies) who had been in their second years the previous season were now signed up as professionals, most of them earning a basic £90 a week. Being old hands at the club, there was a new group of first-years to initiate into the ways of chatting up a mop and to give rowdy encouragement to when the pantomime season came along.

For those who were still eligible, there was their FA Youth Cup title to defend. With most of the previous year's team still available, they were every bit as formidable as before, even if Ryan Giggs was no longer available. In the second round, United beat Blackburn Rovers 4–1 and then moved on to defeat Notts County 3–1. Wimbledon, who had a strong reputation in youth football, were next up and lost 3–0. In the quarter-final, York City were overwhelmed 5–0 to set up a semi-final encounter with Millwall.

For the first leg, Millwall showed they had learned a lesson from their senior colleagues in how to gain a psychological advantage when they all ran on to the Old Trafford pitch with shaven heads. United duly lost the game 2–1, and so had to go to the Den and win. Grant Watts, one of the beaten finalists from Crystal Palace the previous year, remembers that he and a group of his team-mates went along to watch the game at their Southeast London neighbours. It was a close-fought affair, United emerging 2–0 winners to go through 3–2 on aggregate, but Paul Scholes stood out on the night, making Watts realise what strength in depth there was at United. Indeed, Scholes was to be named United youth-team player of the year that season, so much had he progressed.

United's opponents in the final were Leeds United, the club that had pipped the Reds to the league title the previous season. The trans-Pennine rivalry meant that both legs attracted more than 30,000 fans to their respective grounds. In fact, when the Elland Road stadium announcer told the crowd that a few hundred more had turned up for their leg, the volume of noise they created went a notch higher. The first game was played at Old Trafford, but a goal in each half (from Jamie Forrester and Noel Whelan) gave the Yorkshire side a 2–0 advantage. Forrester (with a superb overhead strike) put his team firmly in control when he scored the first goal of the second leg. But the Reds were given a lifeline after 30 minutes when Scholes scored from the penalty spot after a foul on Keith Gillespie. However, a couple of minutes later, Matthew Smithard restored Leeds's three-goal cushion and his team went on to win 4–1 on aggregate.

The defeat was a surprise and a big disappointment, especially given the fact so many had played their part the previous year. Alex Ferguson had said of this side: 'I have never seen their like before.' There weren't many changes from the 1992 final. Darren Whitmarsh had taken over in goal instead of Kevin Pilkington, who was now too old for the competition. At left-back, George Switzer was no longer eligible and his place had gone to Steven Riley; otherwise the defence remained unchanged, with Gary Neville now captain alongside Chris Casper and John O'Kane at right-back. In midfield, David Beckham had moved into the centre alongside Nicky Butt to accommodate Keith Gillespie on the right, while Ben Thornley was still causing chaos on the left. Up front, Scholes and Halifax-born Richard Irving led the line. Robbie Savage came on as a substitute in the first leg and then started in the second after Scholes had to drop back to replace the absent Butt. In both games, Colin Murdock came on for Irving.

For the Class of 92, it was the end of an era – their days of junior football were over. Eric Harrison, who had guided them so far, now had to hand them over to Jim Ryan and the

Reserves as well as to Ferguson. He finally allowed some of his emotions to be revealed. According to Neville, he said after the game: 'You've made me proud.' Beckham, on the other hand, remembers it differently, and says that Harrison went mad at them for losing. Thornley, when asked which version he remembers, can't recall, but adds, 'I'd go with Gaz – he's never wrong!'

There was, however, no doubt about Ferguson's attitude. His message to the players was blunt: 'If you haven't got the temperament, you won't play in my team.' Being a United player was no longer going to be about being a gallant loser; it was about being a winner. As the club had just secured its first league title in 26 years, he wanted to make sure everyone understood that second best wasn't good enough now. Early the following season the two clubs met in the Reserves, fielding very similar sides as in the Youth Cup final, and the Reds won 7–0. It was proof that the manager was right to be very disappointed in the outcome of the tie, feeling they had allowed themselves to be out-muscled.

Although the players were saying farewell to Harrison, the Yorkshireman was already looking to the next generation of youngsters coming through the ranks. In 1995, he managed United to another Youth Cup victory, as they beat Tottenham Hotspur on penalties. By that stage, Phil Neville was the captain of the side, which also featured Terry Cooke, John Curtis, Phil Mulryne and Ronnie Wallwork. When he eventually decided the time had come to take a step back from running the Youth Cup side, as it was a seven-days-a-week role, the manager was having none of it, and persuaded Harrison into looking after the Under-16s.

Soon, however, one of his earliest youth-team graduates, Mark Hughes, was offering him a new challenge. When the former United striker took charge of the Wales national side, Harrison was appointed his assistant manager in August 1999. The Welshman said, 'I have known and respected Eric for many years. He had a major input in my career as well as the likes of Beckham and Giggsy.' When Hughes subsequently moved to take charge of Blackburn Rovers, Harrison also went too. Indeed, he still works for the Lancashire club in a scouting capacity. Since 2002 he has also been employed as head of coaching for the McDonald's community football programme. Working at grass-roots level still gives him immense enjoyment, and it is fair to say that anyone who crosses his path in that role will emerge as a better player and person if they pay attention to what he has to say. After all, can anyone else claim to have trained up quite so many truly great players?

Brian Kidd, who had been such a help to so many of the Class of 92 in their early days, was about to become a very familiar face again. Having moved up to the role of assistant manager in August 1991, he was now one of the men they were anxious to impress if they wanted to get their chance in the senior side. He became an enthusiastic supporter of the idea that they should be given their chance at the highest level, while his presence with the first team made the step up seem rather less daunting than it would otherwise have been.

He remained in the role at Old Trafford until December 1998, when he decided to take on a new challenge and replaced Roy Hodgson as manager of Blackburn Rovers. The club was in a relegation battle when he took charge, but he was unable to turn round their fortunes and they fell out of the Premier League at the end of the season. Sadly, results did not improve the next campaign, and in November 1999 he lost his job.

It wasn't long before he was back in the game, initially working with Leeds United and then taking on the role as Sven-Göran Eriksson's assistant with England in 2003. When he discovered he was suffering from cancer, he stepped down from that role and, after recovering, worked at Sheffield United and then Portsmouth. His next position would take him back to one of his former clubs where he would link up with a former player of his: Mark Hughes at Manchester City. Soon after he arrived, initially to work with the youth team, Hughes was out and he was promoted to become Roberto Mancini's assistant. This latest role gives Kidd a remarkable double, having had significant roles for both Manchester clubs as not only a player but also as an assistant manager.

For the third member of the youth coaching team, Nobby Stiles, his career at United came to an end in 1993. Ferguson had given him additional responsibility as youth development officer after Kidd had moved on from that role. As the manager admitted in his memoirs: 'The job did not suit him and . . . the wee man was parted from the club he loves.' He went on to add, 'I am truly sorry for any pain my wrong decision caused him.' He still remains devoted to the club and lives nearby. As a World Cup winner, Stiles was awarded the MBE in 2000. In autumn 2010, having suffered a mild stroke earlier in the year, he auctioned off his memorabilia, including his World Cup and European Cup medals and shirts, as he felt it was impossible to divide them up between his three children. United stepped in to buy some of the items and the sale raised over £400,000.

For those 1992 winners who were already too old for Youth Cup football, there were mixed fortunes in 1992–93. Giggs was a virtual ever-present in the first team, missing just one league game in the entire season and scoring nine goals in the title-winning campaign. Not yet 20, he had already made 99 senior appearances for United, had won seven caps for Wales and for the second year in a row he was the PFA Young Player of the Year. He'd even been sent some 3,000 Valentine's Day cards as he had become the pin-up boy of the Premier League. He was very much a part of the senior squad now, joining them in the Irish bar Mulligans that was their regular haunt. Lee Sharpe and, increasingly, Paul Ince were his closest friends at the time, and few argued with the theory that he was the best young player in the country.

Things were not going so well for his friend George Switzer, however. He was unable to break into the first team, with Denis Irwin and Clayton Blackmore ahead of him at left-back. By the end of the season, Ferguson had decided he could afford to let him go, feeling he might not be big enough to make the grade (he was just 5ft 6in). He recalls when he made his announcement to the board about who he was proposing to let go, one of the directors spoke up in Switzer's defence: 'Ah, you're not letting George Switzer go. God, they love him; the crowd love him.' Many of his team-mates felt the same way. Colin McKee says: 'He'd done really well, I thought anyway. I thought he was a top left-back.'

For Switzer, it was a devastating blow, after a decade attached to the club: 'For two weeks, I wouldn't go out or anything; I was just whinging and saying there's nowt left. But the people I had around me were just so strong. They said, "Sod it. It's in the past now. Ten years you were there – you've got the cuttings, souvenirs, tops and all that. Just get on with it now."'

For Switzer, there was a second chance to build a career when he moved to Darlington in July. He was signed by Billy McEwan, who had been tipped off by Ferguson that the left-back was available, and was in the starting line-up at the beginning of the season. Unfortunately, the club got off to the worst possible start, failing to win any of their first 13 league games as they slumped to the bottom of Division Three. By 4 October, McEwan had gone and Alan Murray took charge of the team. Switzer struggled to get in the side under the new boss, who signed another left-back, and did not get another run of games until right at the end of the season, when they won three of their final five fixtures and so crept up to 21st out of 22. He admits he found it difficult being so far from home and the people he knew in Manchester. For the second successive summer, Switzer was given a free transfer.

This time, there were no Football League clubs willing to sign him up, so he moved instead to Hyde United of the Northern Premier (Unibond) League. He played for them for six seasons and describes his period with the club as 'brilliant'. Then he got a hernia, which caused him problems over a period of two years, so he moved on to a series of other smaller non-league clubs. When interviewed about his career path in 2000, he said: 'Obviously I'd have liked to be earning the big dollars, and flash cars and that, but I'm happy now the way I am. That's the way I look at it. I don't want to keep looking back, because loads of people have said: "Are you gutted?" No, always look on the bright side of life.'

In November 2008, he was tracked down by the Norwegian newspaper *Dagbladet*. By that stage, Switzer was working for a courier firm, but he still had happy memories of his time at United. He was playing for a club called Monton (and was still doing so in 2011–12), who play at New Alder Park off Worsley Road, west of Manchester. He recalled how he'd bumped into Giggs a couple of years previously. The former team-mates had gone out together, and Switzer's partner had been astonished that he knew someone so famous. For him, there is always a sense of what might have been – not least because it is a question he is often asked. But Switzer looks on the positive side, and points to his good health, good friends and family – including his son Keenan, who is a promising young footballer. Maybe the son will one day fulfil all the hopes the father came so close to achieving. And there's no doubt that he would love him to play for United should he get the opportunity. Once a Red, always a Red.

Switzer was not the only one to be released that summer. Raphael Burke, Mark Gordon and Lennie Taylor were also let go. When Burke left United, he moved back to his home-town club Bristol City. Unfortunately, his career did not progress there, and after the 1993–94 season he left the club. A potential move to Cologne didn't come to anything, and he returned to the UK to play non-league football. By 1996, he had lost his enthusiasm for the game and hung up his boots, taking up a career in a computing company.

Five years later, someone at his church, hearing about Burke's background, suggested he might like to try football coaching. As he had worked on his badges during his career, the idea appealed, as he realised he missed being out on the field playing football – something he had dreamed of doing when he was a young boy. He set up as a freelance coach, working at after-school clubs, and a new career path opened for him. Soon after, he was approached by Bristol City, who had heard about the work he was doing with local kids, to see if he wanted to work with them, too. Ever since, he has been working with the club's junior academy and at foundation level (the under-eights). This work with schools and the youngsters at Bristol City is something he finds very satisfying: 'I get to play outside every day.' As one who has seen what it takes to succeed, he also has a clear message for his charges: they must have the desire to 'overcome obstacles' if they want to make it, and they must have the 'practice mentality'.

So much pleasure did he get out of coaching that in 2008 he decided to put on a pair of boots as a player again for the first time in more than a decade. He now plays for Carmel United, a team set up by his church, in the Bristol and Avon Football League. The crowds may be a thousand times smaller than at Old Trafford, but he has no regrets as he is doing what he loves and is happy being with his wife and their four children.

For Simon Davies and Colin McKee, they both made the step up to Reserve team football, playing for Jim Ryan.

Neville was also getting his regular first taste of football at this level and he commented in an interview at the time: 'We don't get much time off nowadays. We got a bit of time off last year with Eric Harrison, but Jim Ryan runs us into the ground.' But Ryan was unapologetic: 'Stepping into Reserve team football is the step to playing against men, because Reserve team football is open age. History is littered with boys who could do it at their own age group, but when they stepped up found it impossible.' As yet, however, neither Davies nor McKee could find their way into the first team.

The season had not been such a good one for Savage, either. The young Welshman, who had been one of the first to shine in the 'A' team the previous campaign, was now finding his place as a striker under pressure. Richard Irving, like Harrison, was from the Halifax area, and was doing well in his first year as an apprentice. Meanwhile, Beckham, Gillespie, Scholes and Thornley all offered attacking options of different sorts. Savage felt that some of his contemporaries were being fast-tracked through, while he didn't seem to be progressing in the same way. He continued to work hard at his game and admits he wasn't scoring enough goals as a forward to demand attention.

They all knew that the pressure was constantly on them, not just from within their own hard-working and dedicated group, but also from the younger players coming up behind them (Phil Neville, though two years younger, was already making an impression). They also took note of who the manager was signing for the first team. In Savage's case, Mark Hughes and Brian McClair had been the regular forwards since 1988, but then Ferguson had bought Dion Dublin and then, after his serious injury, he went back into the market for another forward – Eric Cantona. Clearly he had a tough job ahead of him if he was going to get into the team ahead of those players.

In the race to see who would be next to follow Giggs from junior football into the senior side, the Class of 92 did not have long to wait to find out the winner. Occasionally one or two of them would travel with the seniors to experience life in the first-team changing room and to get a glimpse of what being a United player was really all about. Neville found this 'the perfect schooling' and he quickly realised these people were 'fierce competitors and real men'. He was impressed by 'their fire and passion' – not to mention witnessing some explosive clashes between them. Often they would be asked to train with the first-teamers as well, to experience the intensity required at that level even in practice.

The 1992–93 season was only a month old when United had a first-round, first-leg home tie in the UEFA Cup against Torpedo Moscow. It was not a particularly glamorous European night, and a crowd of just under 20,000 turned up to watch an underwhelming 0–0 draw. But late in the game, Ferguson took off Lee Martin and Gary Neville made his first senior appearance for United. He slotted in at right-back, while Denis Irwin moved across to left-back to accommodate him. A new full-back partnership was born.

Almost the only time that Neville touched the ball was to take a throw-in. He launched it into the box and it was cleared comfortably by the Moscow defence. But he discovered after the match what senior football meant: there was no hiding place for anyone, no matter how senior. When

Ferguson came into the changing room, he immediately criticised Gary Pallister for not getting into the box to fight for the throw-in – the big defender should have known that Neville had a long throw on him (he'd seen him play for the youth team often enough, hadn't he?) and might therefore create something from that position. Attention to detail – all the time. Or else.

For Neville, it was a special moment. Whatever happened now, he would always be able to call himself a United player. Having done it once, he wanted more. It also helped him to believe that he belonged at the club. As we have seen, at the Cliff there were different changing rooms for the players according to their position in the club. Previously, Neville wouldn't have dreamed of talking to a senior player such as Hughes unless spoken to first. Now he had taken the first step to breaking down that barrier.

A week later, another of the Class of 92 made the step up to the first XI. Most people might have predicted that the next player to make the transition would be Butt or Thornley, but it was neither of them. The game was an away trip to Brighton to play in the Coca-Cola Cup. Ferguson used it as an opportunity to take a few of the youngsters along for the ride, as the squad flew down to Sussex; Beckham, Butt, Neville and Scholes were all on the trip. However, it was Beckham who got his chance, with 17 minutes remaining, when he came on for Andrei Kanchelskis. As he got out of the dugout, he managed to bang his head. Many players say that their debut goes by so quickly in a haze; for Beckham it was possibly literally true. He doesn't remember doing anything wrong, but afterwards he still received some strong words from the manager. The message was clear: this is only the beginning; don't get comfortable and rest on your laurels; there is much more to achieve.

After their brief glimpse of life at the top, Neville and Beckham were quickly returned to where they came from to continue developing their game. At the time, Harrison gave this assessment of the Londoner to the club's magazine: 'He's more of a ball player and is a playmaker in midfield . . . [and] his outstanding qualities are his control and passing ability.'

It was another couple of months before the next one from the Class of 92 made his step up to the first team. This time it was Nicky Butt, and unlike the other two he got his chance in the Premier League. It was 21 November 1992, and United were up against Oldham Athletic, which gave the former Boundary Park player a special incentive – if he needed one. Butt replaced Paul Ince, thus (as with Beckham) prefiguring the change in the line-up that would take place in the summer of 1995. In a *Guardian* interview in 2005, he spoke about that momentous occasion: 'So long ago I can't remember.'

Ferguson gave a debut to one more member of the Youth Cup side during 1992–93, though before that happened he also introduced Cantona to United. It wouldn't happen immediately, but the maverick genius of the Frenchman was also combined with a work ethic that more than matched that of the Class of 92. When they eventually lined up together, it would make for an almost unstoppable team.

Next it was the turn of one of United's young wingers to make the step up. So far, the Class of 92 had played in the UEFA Cup, the League Cup and Premier League, so it was perhaps appropriate that the third round of the FA Cup should complete the set. As Bury were the visitors to Old Trafford, it might have been local boy Thornley, but instead it was Gillespie who got his chance. Harrison's assessment of him at the time was: 'Keith is a very direct winger – probably one of the quickest players at the club . . . He could do with brushing up on his accuracy, but I'm sure that will all come together with experience.' In those days, the manager didn't rotate his squad as much as he has done more recently, so the Irishman was joining what was essentially a full-strength side to take on their local rivals.

His experience was quite different from his three predecessors, not least because he was on from the start. He remembers that he turned up to Old Trafford without any idea that he might be playing. When Paul Parker asked the manager whether Giggs (who was an injury doubt) was fit, Ferguson replied, gesturing to the Irishman: 'No, but he can play.' As Gillespie recalls, 'That was the way he said it, and I wasn't really sure whether he was taking the mick or not at first.'

But soon Gillespie realised he genuinely was about to make his debut. The game could not have gone any better for him. He was played on the right wing and in the first ten minutes he put over a superb cross for Mike Phelan to head home. In the second half, Cantona played the ball through to him, and 'I jinked, shot and the goalkeeper should've saved it, but it went in'. His description of the goal is very modest, for it involved a good run down the wing before he beat his defender and, in the space he created, he had time to drill it hard at the goal and the keeper could only parry it into the roof of the net. He had undoubtedly been the star performer in the match. Afterwards, with United having won 2–0, Gillespie went back to his digs and rang his family back in Northern Ireland to tell them all that had happened – they'd all been listening to the game on the radio, and his goal had been greeted with wild celebrations.

For the rest of the season, neither Gillespie nor any of the other youngsters got a game, as Ferguson kept a very settled first team wherever possible: eight players made 40-plus appearances in the Premier League that season, and Cantona missed just two matches after his signing in December. The result of having such a consistent side, with few injury problems, was that United won the title by the massive margin of ten points. The question now was whether the Class of 92 were going to be good enough to replace the champions.

While Ferguson was waiting for the youngsters to be ready, he made another hugely significant move in the transfer market, bringing in Roy Keane from Nottingham Forest for a record-breaking fee of £3.75 million. Keane was just 22 at the start of the new season, but he'd made 114 league appearances for Brian Clough's side, scoring at a healthy rate for a midfielder of one goal every five games, and was already a Republic of Ireland international. He was one more barrier to the Class of 92 making their breakthrough. Indeed, for the 1993–94 season, with so many of the apprentices signing professional forms, United found themselves with the biggest professional squad in the country.

In 1993–94, Ferguson's policy was again to keep the side as settled as possible. Even in the cup competitions, he rarely changed the personnel. Neither Gillespie nor Beckham was given a second chance in the first team during the season. Butt made two substitute appearances, though both were in significant games: he came on during United's 2–1 Premier League home win against Tottenham Hotspur on 16 October, replacing Giggs, as the manager was keen to give him some experience and as a reward for some fine performances in the Reserves; and he got a second chance when he replaced Parker in extra time in the FA Cup semi-final against Oldham Athletic (already they must have seemed familiar foes to him). He had a significant impact on the game in the short time he was on and was even involved in the move that created Hughes's last-gasp equaliser to take the tie to a replay.

Meanwhile, Neville got his first start in the last Premier League game of the season, when Parker was rested ahead of the FA Cup final. However, it was his previous appearance that season, in the European Cup, which proved to be a real eye-opener. His selection also spoke volumes for the manager's faith in his temperament. Ferguson often took the youngsters to travel with the squad to European matches, so Neville wasn't expecting too much when he travelled to Turkey for the second leg of the second-round tie with Galatasaray. The manager liked to do this because, as he commented at the time: 'Some are more ready than others, and I feel that some first-team experiences will do them no harm.'

It nearly turned out much worse than that. The atmosphere in Istanbul was unlike anything Neville had ever encountered before, with flares going off and deafening chanting for more than an hour before kick-off. Banners saying 'Welcome to Hell' and 'Manchester United RIP' suggested this was not going to be the easiest night. And so it proved. He eventually came on for Phelan with about five minutes to go and the game tied at 0–0, with United needing to win to go through, which they ultimately failed to do.

The encounter ended in controversy: Cantona was sent off, and as he went down the tunnel he was hit by a policeman's baton. Incensed, he tried to find the culprit and had to be dragged to safety by his team-mates, who had to keep watch over him in the changing room to ensure he didn't charge out again to seek vengeance. These events may have been unexpected, but the hostile atmosphere wasn't. Neville was clearly viewed as a young player who could handle it.

The 1993–94 season was also the period when Neville began to make his mark as a right-back, moving across from the centre of defence. Reserve team manager Ryan and his assistant Bryan 'Pop' Robson pointed out to him that while Gary Pallister and Steve Bruce rarely missed a game, Parker at right-back was beginning to pick up a series of injuries. They advised him that if he wanted to make a breakthrough into the first team, that looked to be his best bet. Having begun his United career as a central midfielder, Neville had finally discovered the role that he would make his own for more than a decade. Furthermore, in Irwin he had the perfect role model to learn from when it came to the full-back's art.

The next member of the Class of 92 to get their first taste of action with the senior side was Ben Thornley, who had continued to impress in the Reserves. He came on for the injured Irwin in the Premier League match at Upton Park on 26 February 1994, getting his chance because both Giggs and Sharpe were missing from the side that day. It was a game when little seemed to click for the Reds, but a late Ince equaliser (after his every touch had been booed by the West Ham fans) saved a point in a 2–2 draw.

Thornley remembers the game well, even if it was what happened before he got on that stands out: 'I'd spent sixty-five to seventy minutes on the touchline warming up and it's very close to the fans. I've got [reserve goalkeeper] Les Sealey next to me, arguing with people in the front row about how much money he's earning, and I just wanted to get on. I'd worked hard; this was the moment I'd been waiting for. And to hear Alex Ferguson saying at the end of the game "Well done" to a lad of eighteen on your debut – it just gives you that extra lift.' He also loved the fact that United were playing in his favourite black away kit that day.

A few weeks later, on 6 April, Thornley was under consideration for the FA Cup semi-final tie, because Giggs was struggling with an injury. Then, playing in a Reserve team game against Blackburn, Thornley was on the receiving end of a horrible-looking tackle from Nicky Marker, which resulted in him tearing his cruciate ligaments and put him out of the game for a year. He says of that moment, 'I'm not bitter and I don't have hang-ups, but it ruined my chance.'

Harrison recalls the moment it happened: 'It still sends shivers down my spine when I see the injury and see him carried off. I went to see him in the medical room and he was broken-hearted. I was broken-hearted as well. But for that injury, who knows, I'm sure he would have been an international along with all the rest.' A few weeks later, when the Reserves won the Pontin's League, it was decided that Thornley should be the one to receive the trophy to acknowledge his superb efforts during the campaign. It was another small example of the United family pulling together when one of their own needed support.

Butt, who did get on for the FA Cup game, is of a similar view: 'In my opinion, he was one of the top two players in the youth teams. He was a flair player and everyone liked watching him. Then, all of a sudden, one tackle and he gets knocked back two or three years.'

The final player to make his debut that season was Colin McKee, who was one of the leading goalscorers in the Reserves. He played in the same team as Neville in the final Premier League game of the season. It was a much-changed side, as Ferguson left out Schmeichel, Parker, Keane, Ince, Giggs, Kanchelskis, Hughes and Cantona, with an eye on the following week's FA Cup final. With the league title already won, and minds perhaps straying to Wembley, it was not an easy game in which to play, as the Reds struggled to find any rhythm in a 0–0 home draw. With only scraps to feed off, McKee was eventually substituted to allow Keane a brief run-out. Little did he realise that his first game for United would also be his last.

That day lingers in McKee's mind. On the Saturday, the day before the game, the manager came up to him and said, 'Don't do anything daft tonight, you're starting tomorrow.' At first he thought his fellow Scot was winding him up, but soon realised that his dream was about to come true. He comments: 'You tell someone you've made your debut with Eric Cantona – it doesn't really get any better than that, does it?' In fact, it did, because United were presented with the league trophy at the end of the game, so McKee got to be in the pictures when the presentation was made.

The Class of 92 Graduate to Senior Football

While everyone from the Class of 92 was obviously desperate to get their chance in the first team at United, there was another way to get a taste of senior action: going out on loan. McKee had been the first of the FA Youth Cup-winning side to have this opportunity, when he went to Bury for a brief spell from 8 January 1993 and played a couple of games for the Division Three side managed by Mike Walsh. He found it a character-building experience: his first game was a trip down to Torquay, where they had to set off at 4 a.m., and when he got there the local defenders 'kicked lumps out of you – it toughens you up'.

The following season, on 17 December, Simon Davies was loaned out, this time to Division Two strugglers Exeter City, where Alan Ball was in charge. Although Davies was on the score-sheet on his league debut, helping the Grecians to a 2–2 draw, things did not go well for the rest of his spell there. On the day that Sir Matt Busby died, 20 January 1994, Ball left Exeter to take charge of Southampton and a few days later Terry Cooper took over. In the other five games Davies played for them, Exeter lost them all and failed to score a single goal. It was all a very different experience from what he was used to at United, where winning was the norm and all the facilities were of the highest quality.

Gillespie also went out on loan during the 1993–94 season, heading off to Wigan Athletic on 3 September. It seems strange to consider that in those days they were in the bottom division, too. But the Irishman continued to impress and scored four goals in eight games at the Latics under Kenny Swain.

Though progress to the senior side had been slower than

they would have liked, the Class of 92 recognised the talent that was ahead of them in the United squad, who as Double winners in 1994 were clearly the best team in the country. Unfortunately, the end of the season was the end of the road at United for two more of those who had played their part in winning the Youth Cup. It was two of the Youth Cup side's strikers who were on their way out: Joe Roberts and Robbie Savage.

Roberts was given only a short-term professional contract when his apprenticeship ended in 1993, while he remembers that eight of the others received a four-year deal, including a £20,000 signing-on fee, £5,000 payable each year. It amused him to think that if any of them had been kept on their original deal, four years later they would have been getting a meagre £5,000 bonus for winning the Double in 1996.

After leaving United, he had a trial at Leeds United and then received an offer from Sheffield United, then managed by Dave Bassett. But the terms were so poor, he took up an option to play in Finland for GBK Kokkola, where he was offered a three-year contract. However, because their season did not start until the following spring, he was free to play non-league football at Witton Albion until April 1995. His spell in Finland was going well until he tore his ankle ligaments and that injury put him out of the game for 18 months.

His playing career never fully recovered from that setback, and so he played on for non-league Witton Albion, where Beckham's good friend Dave Garland also played, so the Cheshire club would sometimes have some very starry supporters in their midst. After Witton, Roberts played on at

Winsford United, but the amount of travelling involved, when he had a young family to consider, meant he soon decided to play at a lower level where he would not have to travel all over the country on very meagre pay. Middlewich, who played in the Cheshire League, were his next club because the bulk of their fixtures took place in that county.

A meeting with comedian John Bishop's brother soon led to a new career as a window cleaner, and he now runs his own business in Cheshire employing several people. He looks back on his time at United with great fondness – as well as a shocking confession. He says he has no regrets about how things panned out for him, and then admits to one: 'I only wish I'd played at Anfield.' A Liverpool fan (news that came as a surprise to most of his former team-mates), Roberts almost got his chance when he was due to play there, having just scored six goals against Bolton in an 'A' team game. However, the club decided they wanted him to play in a Lancashire Youth Cup game against Blackburn Rovers instead – so he missed his chance. To make matters worse, when he got to Blackburn he found himself on the bench and didn't play.

He also had a ready answer one day in 2002 when he was sitting in a bar and someone asked the inevitable question: where did it all go wrong? England were playing in the World Cup and he pointed up at the screen, where Beckham, Butt and Scholes were all in action, and Gary Neville missed out only through injury. 'I was up against half the England side,' he commented. It was a fair point.

Meanwhile, Savage had been given only a one-year professional contract at the start of 1993–94, so when he was called in to see the manager at the end of the campaign, he was hopeful that he might be given another 12 months in which to prove himself. He admits that he had struggled during the season, as he had suffered from a double hernia that kept him out of action for four months. Instead of getting the chance to impress Ryan in the Reserve team, he had spent much of his time working with physio Jim McGregor and Jimmy Curran on trying to get back to fitness. When he had finally recovered, the season was half gone. Feeling that he had to impress at every step, he was unable to deliver the kind of performances that would secure his future. He hoped the mitigating factor of his injury problems would result in him getting another chance.

Sadly for Savage, Ferguson had to consider the bigger picture. From his point of view, United had a range of superb strikers already competing for places in the first team, and among the younger group there was also McKee and Scholes. It was hard to see where Savage could fit in. For the manager, it was one of the most difficult and painful parts of his job – releasing talented, committed young players who had done nothing wrong. The manager told him he'd been 'fantastic' and gave him these words of encouragement: 'You will make it somewhere. One day you will come back to haunt me.'

If that news was bad enough, Savage's day was about to get much worse. He drove home to Wales still in shock and when he swerved to avoid an animal that had run out on to the road, he crashed straight into an oncoming car. Fortunately, the driver in the other car eventually made a full recovery, while Savage was kept in hospital for three days. It could have been much more serious.

While Savage lay in his hospital bed, the club sent him flowers and the United chaplain paid him a visit – he was still treated as part of the family even though he had left – but he also vowed to set out on a mission to prove Ferguson wrong. Already Dario Gradi at Crewe had been in touch. It was the club he had rejected before, but now they saw their opportunity, and for him it was a chance to get on the road back to the top. It was a path David Platt had also taken: United reject, Crewe revival, international success.

Initially, that all seemed highly ambitious. Savage did not feel entirely settled at Crewe; he made just six appearances in his first season and 30 the next campaign. But it was during that 1995–96 season that Bobby Gould decided to try something different with Savage when he was playing for the Wales Under-21 side. Gould realised the youngster had neither the pace nor the physical presence to be a great centre-forward. What he did have was seemingly limitless energy; the sort of player ideally suited for a midfield role. The switch worked: having made his debut for Wales on 15 November in attack against Albania, by the end of the season he was being used in midfield in a friendly against Switzerland. Even now, Harrison says he was surprised that the switch worked so well, as he admits he did not see that potential in the Welshman, who had come to United as an out-and-out striker.

After another season at Crewe, Savage was transferred to Leicester City in the summer of 1997 for a fee of £400,000. Playing for manager Martin O'Neill in the Premier League, Savage now had his chance to make Ferguson's prediction come true. On 31 January 1998, he was in action at Old

Trafford and helped the Foxes record a surprise 1–0 win. He admits he enjoyed going back to Old Trafford: 'You can have a little banter [with your old team-mates] . . . And to go there and win, having been released, is special.' Had United even drawn that game, they and not Arsenal would have won the league.

He stayed at the East Midlands club until the summer of 2002, when he moved to Birmingham City after the Foxes were relegated. This time his fee was £1.25 million, and while there he ended up playing for a former United colleague in Steve Bruce. In early 2005, he moved to Blackburn Rovers in a controversial £3.1 million transfer deal, where he linked up with another ex-United player in Mark Hughes. After spending three years at Blackburn, he moved on to his final club, Derby County, in January 2008. The season ended in relegation, but after being a regular in his first season, he was on the edge of things in 2008–09 until Nigel Clough was appointed manager and brought Savage back into his side.

In a period of little more than six weeks from the start of the New Year, Savage would line up against his original club three times. Initially came the first leg of the Carling Cup semi-final on 7 January at Pride Park, the day after Clough joined, and the new manager saw his side win 1–0. Savage was only a substitute in the game, but his former team-mate Scholes lined up against him. At Old Trafford two weeks later, both Giggs and Neville were in the side as the Reds eased to a 3–0 lead in just 34 minutes. With the game seemingly over, Savage came on at half time and he galvanised the Rams to score two late goals, but a further strike for the Reds saw United win through to the final 4–3 on aggregate. In mid-February, the two sides were paired up again, this time in the fifth round of the FA Cup, but this was a much more straightforward affair for United, who won through 4–1.

At the end of the 2010–11 season, Savage finally retired from the game. By then he had played more than 600 senior games and won 39 caps for Wales (it would surely have been more, but he retired from international football in 2005). He has begun to develop a career in broadcasting, working for Radio 5 live. He is enjoying his media career: 'I love football, and I love talking about football, so going into the media to talk about it was great.' He also took part in the 2011 series of *Strictly Come Dancing*, managing to break his nose during one spectacular move. In a subsequent spin-off event, Eric Harrison was in the audience to see him perform. Savage expected nothing less than an honest verdict from his old boss, as 'he always used to tell the truth'.

Given Savage's rejection by United in 1994, he could be justifiably proud of a superb career, built on hard work and dedication, as well as some occasional pantomime villainy that was usually much more in jest than anything else. If this was what one of the 'rejects' could do, just what did the future hold for the rest of the Class of 92?

10

No Way Through for Some

'I always did just enough, and at United you can't do that. You've got to work your nuts off, basically.'

John O'Kane

After winning back-to-back league titles, United went into the 1994–95 season as favourites to complete a hat-trick. Sure, there was a new rival in Blackburn Rovers, where Jack Walker's millions were helping to transform the nature of the game in England. For the first time a club owner had decided to spend major amounts of money in search of honours – he would not be the last to do so. In July 1994, Rovers had signed Chris Sutton for a UK record transfer of £5 million and were paying him a reported salary of £12,000 a week. Managed by Kenny Dalglish, they were sure to be serious challengers in the season ahead.

For the remaining members of the Class of 92 still at United, the good news was that there was only one significant summer signing at Old Trafford: David May, an adaptable defender who could slot in at either centre-back or full-back. This was in recognition that, at 33, Steve Bruce couldn't be expected to go on forever at the heart of United's defence alongside Gary Pallister. With Bryan Robson and Mike Phelan having left the club, Alex Ferguson had been signalling from the end of the previous campaign that he expected to use the youngsters more often this time round.

There was another important change that was to emerge in the thinking of the manager during this season. Previously, Ferguson had consistently played his first-choice team whenever possible, though he had rotated his squad somewhat for the Coca-Cola Cup ties against Stoke City. He had taken this approach a step further for the last league fixture of the previous campaign, ahead of the FA Cup final, and been rewarded with a 4–0 win at Wembley. Now, with the European Cup being transformed into the Champions League, creating a heavier workload, he realised that he might have to change things around a little bit more than he had done before. As early as May 1994, he was signalling the way he was thinking: 'I will certainly play the younger players in the Coca-Cola Cup without any qualms. They won't let me down.'

By now, the level of interest in the younger players coming through the club's ranks was beginning to increase. *Manchester United* magazine reflected much of this at the time, with senior players regularly asked for their opinions on the future generation and brief profiles given to some of them. From the

Class of 92, Ryan Giggs was inevitably a regular entry in there already, but, him apart, the September 1994 issue saw the first player from that group to be given the double-page pull-out poster treatment. It wasn't David Beckham or Nicky Butt or Gary Neville who was the first pin-up – it was goalkeeper Kevin Pilkington. The same edition also featured a picture of United's first-team squad for 1994–95, and only Butt and Chris Casper featured as a part of the line-up. There was still little sense at that time who the future stars would be pre-ordained.

Meanwhile, as he'd promised he would, in September (after a run of games against Leeds United, Gothenburg and Liverpool beforehand) Ferguson decided to play an experimental side in the first leg of the second round of the Coca-Cola Cup, when United travelled to Vale Park. His selection for the game against First Division Port Vale on 21 September 1994 was hugely controversial. Simon Davies, John O'Kane and Paul Scholes were all given debuts, O'Kane as a substitute. Beckham, Butt, Keith Gillespie and Gary Neville were also selected. In total, seven out of the Class of 92, with only a handful of senior appearances between them, lined up that night.

The manager was accused of disrespecting the League Cup. He recalls some of the controversy: 'We were getting letters from MPs, demands to be thrown out of the cup and all the rest of it – and we won. Can you imagine if we'd got beat?' It had seemed they might suffer that fate when Lee Glover scored for the Valiants in the first minute or so. Fortunately, the Reds were soon back in it – and it was one of the debutants who scored.

The equaliser came when the Port Vale left-back attempted to play a pass to his team-mate in the centre of defence. Cleverly anticipating the ball, United's forward nipped in to intercept and then beat Paul Musselwhite, chipping the ball over the 6ft 2in keeper. Paul Scholes had scored his first goal for United. After the break, he doubled his tally when Butt crunched into a tackle in the midfield. The loose ball was picked up by Brian McClair, who spread it out wide to the left to Davies. The Welshman bamboozled his defender before putting over a great cross, and Scholes got above his marker to head into the corner from eight yards out.

It was an extremely assured performance from the youngsters, and it had the travelling supporters chanting: 'They go to school in the morning and Choccy is their teacher.' Afterwards, a delighted Ferguson commented, 'They didn't seem to have a care and feared no one.' The press, who had been so critical beforehand, now shifted tack dramatically: 'Nothing like it since Matt Busby's glorious era,' said the *Sun*, while *Today* added that Beckham 'will surely follow the route of Ryan Giggs'.

For the second leg, Ferguson kept faith with his youngsters, even though controversy still dogged his selection policy. At Old Trafford, he gave a debut to Casper (as well as to 18-year-old new signing Graeme Tomlinson), while Beckham, Butt, Davies, Gillespie, Neville, O'Kane and Scholes were also in the line-up. At the age of 20, Davies was the fifth oldest in the side, with eight teenagers playing their part. This time it was two of the senior members – McClair and May – who scored the goals, but the kids of United had come through their first senior trial with flying colours. The

Daily Mirror was sure it had seen 'the shape of things to come'.

The manager explained the logic of his thinking as follows: 'It's a fallacy of the youth programme, if the manager has not got the commitment to it, it means nothing. A scout can scout him and bring him to the club; a youth coach can develop him, put him in the Reserve team; the Reserve team coach can help him on his way and recommend him for the first team, but if the manager'll not play him in the first team it's a waste of blinking time as far as I'm concerned.' Davies puts it stronger than that. To him, it wasn't commitment, but Ferguson (like Busby before him) was 'brave to give youth its chance' when his job could be on the line if things went wrong.

Ferguson continued to trust in youth in the third round of the Coca-Cola Cup, but the opposition was much more formidable this time round, as United travelled up to St James' Park to take on Newcastle United. Having just beaten Blackburn three days before in the league, and with another game against the Magpies due three days later, followed by a trip to Barcelona after that, it made sense to continue with the experiment. Beckham, Butt, Davies, Gillespie, Neville and Scholes were all selected this time, but could not prevent the Reds from losing 2–0 when they succumbed to two late goals as tiredness crept in. Despite that, the *Daily Express* marvelled at 'the sweet, uninhibited football of Fergie's Fledglings'.

When so many clubs these days field weakened sides for cup competitions, it is hard to conceive just how unusual these moves from Ferguson were at the time. But in fact they were revolutionary. He was the first to grasp the importance of giving his players an occasional rest and he understood that having a large squad of first-team quality players would mean United could cope better than their rivals in an injury crisis. It helped that he had a group of youngsters coming through who knew all about playing the United way, and who were clearly highly talented. Playing them at senior level was the final test of their temperament.

At the time, it seemed to some commentators as though he was just giving a bunch of kids a run-out to spare his first team. But that was because those looking on did not know just how significant many of those players would be to United's future. As Ferguson wrote in his memoirs: 'I have never been so positive about a group of young footballers . . . Their promise . . . put the club in its strongest position since my arrival.' His main concern was that 'young players of exceptional ability fly on gossamer wings', and so one has to ensure they don't play too much and burn out or get over-exposed. Guiding Giggs to more than 900 appearances shows the rewards for getting it right.

However, even after this mass experiment, there was still one member of the Class of 92 who had yet to make his senior debut. Fortunately, Pilkington did not have much longer to wait. He was on the bench at Old Trafford when United took on Crystal Palace on 19 November, and when Peter Schmeichel's back injury flared up, he finally got his chance in goal after just seven minutes of the game. It was fortunate for him that his debut came unexpectedly, because there was no time for nerves to creep in. He kept a clean sheet in the Reds' impressive 3–0 victory that took them to the top of the table. However, it wasn't a game entirely without incident for him. At one stage he came rushing off his line to claim the ball, and as he did so slid close to the edge of the box. Some Palace players claimed he had carried the ball out of his area and that he should be sent off for deliberate handball. Fortunately, the referee did not see things that way and Pilkington stayed on the pitch. When he went home afterwards, he remembers how his family were so 'made up' that he'd made his debut, and how proud everyone was that he was now officially a United player. By the end of the season, Jim Ryan had named him the Player of the Year in the Reserves after what he described as an 'out-standing' season.

Davies remembers that game, too, as it was his Premier League debut. For him the thing that he recalls was standing in the tunnel, waiting to run on to the Old Trafford pitch. He was stood in line behind Gary Pallister, so 'I can hear things, but I can't see anything' because the giant defender was blocking his view.

However, the 1994–95 season was no longer just about giving the youngsters an occasional run-out. Some of them were now becoming much more regular picks in the side. It was Butt (22 starts and 13 substitute appearances), Neville (23 plus four) and Scholes (ten plus 15, with seven goals) who led the way. As predicted, injuries to Paul Parker had left him very much on the periphery, which enabled Neville to have a couple of longer runs in the side. All three of them played in every one of the final six league games of the campaign, as United tried to reel in Blackburn, who stuttered towards the finishing line, picking up just seven points in their final six fixtures. It was still enough to see them home by a point when United failed to beat West Ham United in the last game of the season.

There had been one significant change during the season. The arrival of Andrew Cole from Newcastle, in a deal valued at £7 million, had seen Gillespie sent in the opposite direction on 10 January. Ferguson was reluctant to let the young winger from Northern Ireland go, but the Magpies had insisted. He had scored a great goal against them in the league that had caught manager Kevin Keegan's eye. The first Gillespie heard about the possible deal was the day before the move went through, during United's FA Cup third-round game at Sheffield United. Ferguson had a word with him in the Bramall Lane toilets, when he explained what was on offer. That evening, they met up with Keegan and the deal was done, with the Geordie boss commenting: 'He's possibly the best youngster I've seen in the game since I came back. Keith could become the best of his generation.'

For a while, it seemed as though the Reds might regret his departure. Indeed, when Andrei Kanchelskis was sold at the end of the season, there was even media speculation that United might try to re-sign him, but Ferguson was to look elsewhere for someone to play on the right flank. For Gillespie, there was the consolation of being a much more regular starter at Newcastle. His abundant promise was fulfilled on a glorious night when he tore apart the Barcelona defence and showed just how good a player he could be.

Gillespie stayed on Tyneside until 15 December 1998, making 143 appearances for the Magpies, when he was sold for a fee of £2.35 million. His new club was Blackburn Rovers, where he linked up once again with Brian Kidd, who had taken over as manager there less than a fortnight before. The pair were unable to prevent Rovers from being relegated, which eventually cost Kidd his job. Gillespie stayed on, but was loaned out to Wigan during 2000–01, before returning to help Blackburn win the League Cup in 2002. A year later, he moved on to Leicester City in the summer of 2003 after making 113 league appearances for Rovers.

As someone who had seemed to offer such a goal threat, Gillespie was a surprisingly sporadic scorer by now. He stayed in the East Midlands until 2005, after which he signed for Sheffield United. Having been a regular pick up to the end of 2007–08, the next season he found himself out of favour and was loaned out to Charlton Athletic before signing for Bradford City in 2009. After that, apart from a brief spell at Darlington, he returned to Northern Ireland, playing initially for Glentoran and then for Longford Town. It was a career that saw him play a total of 396 league games, scoring 27 goals. He also made an impressive 86 appearances for Northern Ireland between 1994 and 2008. Only Mal Donaghy (91), David Healy (89 to date) and Sammy McIlroy (88) – all with United connections – among outfield players have played more often for their country.

Yet despite this incredible record, some still feel that he might have achieved even more. If he had stayed at United, the chances are he would have been a squad player, with Giggs and Beckham taking the wide midfield positions, and it is hard to see anyone being satisfied with that role in the long run. More pertinently, in October 2010 he was declared bankrupt, having built up a series of debts through his heavy gambling. 'Everybody says it's a mug's game . . . A lot of that back then was due to being naïve, being young and a little bit of boredom,' he explained. Although, as we have seen, he had started gambling at United, it was while he was living in a hotel in Newcastle that it became a more serious issue. He commented, 'There's only so much that clubs can do for you, you're your own person; I got involved in gambling and that's my problem ... It's in your make-up and your personality, and it did pass the time and it didn't go too well.'

A few weeks after Gillespie was allowed to leave United, one other player was worried that he might be following him out of Old Trafford when he was loaned to Preston North End for a month from 28 February 1995. His last appearance in a red shirt had been in the Champions League at Old Trafford back in early December, when he had scored his first senior goal for the club against Galatasaray. Since then, he hadn't played for United, and had begun to notice that others from the Class of 92 were getting their chance more frequently than he was. So when David Beckham was told he was going to Preston, he wondered if he was being eased out. After he'd been given the news, he discussed the situation with Eric Harrison and soon after was invited back in to see Ferguson. The manager reassured him that there was nothing more sinister behind it than giving him the opportunity to have some first-team football.

Beckham was still developing physically at the time, so the chance to play a few matches in Division Three, where the game could often be more robust than in the Premier League, turned out to be a great opportunity. Given that message from the manager, Beckham threw himself into things at Preston. As soon as he arrived, the manager told those who normally took corners and penalties that the United teenager would be in charge of them while he was there. It might have caused resentment, but his commitment to the cause eased any possible tension. With club captain David Moyes ensuring the players supported him, Beckham found himself loving his time at the club. He also got to recognise just how vital success was at the lower level, when money from win bonuses could make all the difference and mortgage payments could often depend on them. Beckham's positive impact on the club's results made him a popular member of the changing room. Indeed, he enjoyed it so much that he even asked if he could stay for another month, but Ferguson said no.

The spell at Deepdale seems to have helped Beckham mature, toughen up and grow in confidence. After he returned to Old Trafford, he soon found himself getting a run in the first team. As he has commented: '[Ferguson] believes in the lads who have grown up at the club.' What was more, Beckham now felt he belonged at this level, too. His Premier League debut came against Leeds at Old Trafford – it was a big game, but manager and player felt ready for it.

While Beckham had been given the chance to develop his game at another club, there was one other member of the Class of 92 who was let go at the beginning of the season. Having made his debut at the end of the 1993–94 season, Colin McKee was sold to Kilmarnock early the following campaign. He'd been doing well in the Reserves, and the manager told him that the SPL side had watched him a few times and made the club an offer, which United were happy to accept. Ferguson left McKee to talk with Kilmarnock and to make his decision. In the end, the appeal of first-team football won through, and McKee returned to Scotland. He recognised that his chances of getting a game weren't going to be helped by the UEFA eligibility limits then in place for European competitions that meant English teams needed plenty of English players, a ruling that had helped some of the Class of 92 to have an opportunity.

McKee settled in quickly at the Ayrshire SPL side, making 25 league appearances in his first season at the club, and ending up as the leading scorer with six goals. The following campaign, McKee made 28 SPL appearances, but scored only four goals and found himself increasingly on the bench or utilised on the wing. In 1996–97, almost half of his 25 games in the SPL came from the bench, and he scored just twice, so in October 1997 he was released by Kilmarnock when a knee injury kept him out of the game for 18 months. Because of this, it took him a while to find a new club, before he eventually signed for Falkirk. But his knee was never quite right again, and he picked up other injuries, including a broken collarbone and a broken arm, so in 2001 he called it a day and retired from the game. It was 'one injury after another', he recalls.

After that he moved into coaching, working with a former Kilmarnock team-mate, Paul Wright, and eventually they found themselves coaching the Under-17s at their old club. Working with the youth team there, he remembered many of the lessons he had learned from Harrison when he had been that age. He'd provided 'discipline from an early age, but everything he was doing was to make you a better person'. He says the hardest part of it all was letting people go when the time came to decide who should be offered professional contracts. He remembers one year where he had 18 apprentices, but only three were kept on. It again highlights just how special United's 1991 intake was: every single one of them was offered a contract at the end of their apprenticeship.

In 2008, McKee decided to focus his attention on his young son and to coach his team. Now nine, the boy knows what career he wants and who he wants to play for. Earlier in the 2011–12 season, they went to Old Trafford together for the first time and, at the interval, 'my wee boy says, "When I'm playing for Man United, I'll get you this every week."' As well as his coaching, he is also working in the building and maintenance trade.

While 1994–95 had seen some members of the Class of 92 begin to establish themselves in the first team, others had been moved on. For those in between – players such as Casper, Davies, O'Kane, Pilkington and Thornley – there was all to play for. Just how true that was became clear when United won the Youth Cup again in May, beating Tottenham Hotspur 4–3 on penalties at Old Trafford after the two legs of the final had finished 2–2 on aggregate. From within the ranks of that team, Phil Neville had already made his senior debut. The Class of 92 were no longer the youngest prospects, there were others coming through as well. The question for this group now was whether they could make a slightly belated breakthrough, or would they have to move on to a new club. The fact that the manager sold three senior players during the summer of 1995 without buying any replacements at least ensured they would have a chance.

The 1995–96 campaign saw United go on to complete the double Double, inspired by the return of Cantona after his eight-month ban for assaulting a foul-mouthed Crystal Palace fan. Beckham, Butt, Giggs and Gary Neville were all now pretty much established as first-choice players, with Phil Neville and Scholes not too far behind them. For Pilkington, however, there was good news when second-choice keeper Gary Walsh decided to move on to Middlesbrough, frustrated at the lack of first-team opportunities he was getting. This meant Pilkington was now effectively Peter Schmeichel's back-up, and so he made five appearances during the season. However, with the Dane rated by many to be the best in the world, it was clear the young keeper was only ever going to get his chance when Schmeichel was rested or injured. To get more experience, he went to Rochdale on loan for a month in February.

If he hoped he was being lined up as the Dane's long-term successor, Pilkington was disappointed when Ferguson signed Raimond van der Gouw from Vitesse Arnhem in the summer of 1996. The experienced Dutchman was 33 and had played more than 350 games in the Netherlands. During 1996–97 whenever Schmeichel was absent, it was van der Gouw who took his place. Unsurprisingly in the circumstances, Pilkington went out on loan again, this time to Rotherham United, staying there from the beginning of February to the end of the season.

Things improved slightly for Pilkington in 1997–98, when he made two more appearances for United, but he was again loaned out. At the end of the season, he decided it was time to move on, and went to Port Vale on a free transfer. Even playing one division lower, Pilkington still found himself a second-choice keeper. After 23 games in two seasons, Pilkington left the Valiants and during 2000–01 it seemed as if he might be drifting out of the game, as he struggled to settle at Macclesfield Town, Wigan Athletic and Mansfield Town.

But in 2001–02, at the age of 27, he was finally given the opportunity his talent had suggested he had always deserved, when he became Mansfield's regular keeper. It may have been at the bottom tier of the Football League, but he helped his side to promotion. He remembers they were playing against Carlisle United and the fans were gathered round the edge of the pitch, waiting to come on to celebrate. The biggest fear he had was that they would encroach on the field and the referee would abandon the game, but happily the day ended in celebrations. They came straight back down, but in 2003–04 they reached the play-off final at the Millennium Stadium and when the game ended 0–0 after extra time, promotion had to be decided on a penalty shoot-out. Coincidentally, his opposite number for Huddersfield Town was another former United keeper, Paul Rachubka. Sadly for Pilkington, it was the latter who triumphed.

After another solid season at Mansfield, Pilkington was offered reduced terms on his contract and decided to move to Notts County. He stayed in the East Midlands until 2010, experiencing that club's period of turmoil, but eventually found himself battling with first Russell Hoult and then Kasper Schmeichel for the goalkeeper's jersey. Having previously lost out to the father, finding himself behind the son as he approached his 36th birthday was surely the last thing he wanted at that stage of his career. As he comments, it was 'very surreal'. Unsurprisingly, he met up again with Peter Schmeichel during that time and the Dane said to him, 'You must hate us.' But, to his credit, that is not his response to the formidable Schmeichel barrier to his career. He says now: 'It was frustrating, but you're learning off the best and that will help you in the long run.'

But Schmeichel *fils* had his own source of inspiration, beyond the advice he got from his father: ironically, it was the Class of 92 who had shown him how to make the most of his career. As he explained in a *Guardian* interview in February 2012: 'I was incredibly lucky when I grew up because ... I saw the best players of their generation train every day.' Watching the likes of Beckham, Giggs and Scholes, as well as Cantona and his father, 'I saw how hard they worked, the perfectionism and the absolute dedication required to reach the top. Their work ethic is the reason they were the best and the reason they, in the case of Giggs and Scholes, still are the best.'

During the 2009–10 season Pilkington went out on loan to Blue Square Premier League side Luton Town, and at the end of the season made the move a permanent one. In 2010–11, he was loaned back to Mansfield, who had joined Luton in the Blue Square Premier League. In 2011–12, he continued to play for Luton – one of the few members of the Class of 92 still in action anywhere – and had also begun to focus on coaching, starting at Ilkeston. With almost 450 senior appearances behind him, Pilkington had proved himself an enduring product of the Class of 92. In February 2012, the next stage of his career opened up for him when he returned to Notts County as their goalkeeping coach. While he still hopes there may be the odd call for him to don the gloves again, he recognises that at 38 such moments are coming to an end and that it is now time to focus on the next stage of his career – the one he hopes will see him through the next 20 years. At County he has a 'fantastic opportunity to go back home, with my family and my wife's family all living nearby'.

While Pilkington's route to the first team was always likely to be blocked, because of the nature of the goalkeeper's role, that wasn't true for the rest of the Class of 92. Simon Davies was the one who appeared most likely to be the next one to make the breakthrough, but finding his way into the side was difficult. The former captain of the Youth Cup side had slightly adapted his game, and was now sometimes used on the left side of midfield, rather than playing in the centre. But in either role, he faced fierce competition to get into the side. As it was, after making ten appearances in the previous season, in 1995–96 that number dropped to eight.

The summer of 1996 saw Ferguson enter the market in the most significant way for many years, as he signed up Jordi Cruyff, Ronny Johnsen, Karel Poborský and Ole Gunnar Solskjaer, as well as goalkeeper van der Gouw. Changes to the rules on the use of foreigners in the Champions League (whose numbers had previously been restricted) were behind this mass importation of overseas talent. Whereas previously there had been a need to keep a large pool of English or British players available, that was no longer so important. As a result, in 1996–97, Davies played just two games for United, the last of them in the fourth round of the Coca-Cola Cup on 27 November, when United lost 2–0 at

Leicester City. Casper, O'Kane, Scholes and Thornley also played in that game, as did three other home-grown talents: Michael Appleton, Michael Clegg and Terry Cooke, all of whom were even younger. It was to be Davies's farewell performance for the Reds. Before the season was over, he was sent out on loan to Huddersfield Town.

At the end of the season, it was clear that the time was right for Davies to move on. He was sold to Luton Town for a fee of £150,000 in August 1997, but after a decent start at the Division Two club he soon found himself often on the bench or not picked at all by Lennie Lawrence. In December 1998, he moved to Sammy McIlroy's Macclesfield Town, struggling to avoid relegation from the same division, for an undisclosed fee. He was unable to prevent them going down and indeed missed much of the campaign. Season 1999–2000 was the period that saw him in action the most frequently in his career, as he made 36 league appearances, scoring just once. He moved to Rochdale in the summer of 2000, and played for them for a season. After a career of 102 league appearances for six different clubs, and with six goals to his credit, Davies moved to Bangor City to play in the League of Wales.

Having won a cap for Wales back in April 1996, when he came on as a substitute for Gareth Taylor against Switzerland, this was some sort of homecoming for him. His period in Welsh football took him also to Total Network Solutions and Rhyl before he moved to Chester City in 2006 to begin a career in coaching. After a spell as youth-team coach at the club, he was eventually promoted to manager in March 2008 and was given a two-year contract the following month, just as he turned 34. The club was struggling to stay in the Football League, and in financial difficulties at the time. Despite that, he helped them secure their survival with a draw in the penultimate game of the season. The following campaign, he lost his job at the debt-laden club on 11 November. Although results had not been great, the club was then in 19th place, which was a small improvement and would have been enough to keep them up at the end of the season. Chairman Stephen Vaughan had hoped for more progress, but in the end the club was relegated, and by March 2010 it was wound up. As managerial baptisms of fire go, it was a pretty tough one for Davies. Subsequently, he has moved to a club at the opposite end of the financial scale, and is now working with the Manchester City youth set-up.

John O'Kane was the next member of the Class of 92 to leave Old Trafford, and he also said his farewell to first-team action for United in the Coca-Cola Cup match against Leicester City in November 1996. He made seven appearances in all for the Reds. During the 1996–97 season, he had two loan spells with Bury, making a total of 13 appearances for them, which he says toughened him up. The following campaign, he spent November at Bradford City on loan, and so when Everton manager Howard Kendall offered £250,000 to take him to Goodison Park on 30 January 1998, it made sense to take the new opportunity this presented. By that time, Denis Irwin and the Neville brothers were all regulars in the full-back positions, and John Curtis had emerged as a younger contender for that role. Before the season was out, he had made 12 appearances for the Toffees.

The fact that O'Kane had been the right-back in the Youth Cup side and not Neville has led many to query whether he feels angry about it. O'Kane comments, 'A lot of my mates say, "He has got your career," and I think, no, he worked hard for his career, and at the end of the day I didn't work hard enough ... A lot of us had good skill and so didn't tend to work as hard as he's had to work. But he's a legend in my book – probably one of the best right-backs of all time.'

There were two other differences between them, O'Kane believes: he was an extremely adaptable player, capable of lining up anywhere along the back line and even in midfield, too. As a consequence, he recognises he never fully mastered any one position. Additionally, Neville 'ate and slept football. I didn't particularly like football. It was a job to me. If you don't like a job, you'll not give a hundred per cent and I always did just enough, and at United you can't do that. You've got to work your nuts off, basically.' It is a very honest appraisal of his own career, and reveals as well as anything else what it takes to make it at the highest level.

Sadly for O'Kane, during the summer there was a change of manager at Goodison Park, and new boss Walter Smith seemed to have little use for him. In October, he was loaned out to Burnley for a spell, before returning to make just two appearances for Everton late on in the campaign. The second of them was at Old Trafford where he faced up to Beckham, Butt and the Neville brothers – it was to be his last appearance in a blue shirt. When he came off the field, being substituted near the end, he remembers getting a warm round of applause from the United fans, which was a special moment, knowing that they were saluting one of their own.

In November 1999, Sam Allardyce took him on loan at Bolton Wanderers and the following month the deal was made a permanent one. In 2000–01, he helped the Trotters win promotion back to the Premier League, making 27 appearances. In the summer, Allardyce sold him on to Blackpool, then in Division Two. Under Steve McMahon, O'Kane had the most consistent run of first-team action in his career, making 38 league appearances in all. The former England international made him captain of the side, and they went on to win the LDV Vans Trophy at the Millennium Stadium in Cardiff, beating Cambridge United 4–1. However, O'Kane always found that he quickly became 'stale' at each of his clubs after United, and his relationship with the manager duly suffered.

So at the end of the 2002–03 season he moved to non-league Hyde United, who had just been relegated from the Unibond Premier Division. Coincidentally, his last game for the Seasiders came three days before former Class of 92 team-mate Ben Thornley made his debut at the club. A chance to rekindle old times was lost. Throughout his career, O'Kane made 134 league appearances, scoring nine goals in that time. O'Kane stayed with Hyde until 2006, when he retired from the game at the age of 31. He says now that his time at Hyde was when 'I fell in love with the game again. For the first time in years, I actually enjoyed turning up for a game and playing.' He now works with schools in a job that really fires his enthusiasm and passion in a way that football somehow never quite did. 'It feels like you're doing good,' he concludes.

After O'Kane, it was Thornley who was the next to leave

Old Trafford. In truth, the winger had never fully recovered from the cruciate ligament injury he received on 6 April 1994. It wasn't until February 1995 that he was able to start making his way again in the Reserves and, as he admitted at the time, he had piled on some extra weight in the interim. There is no doubt that losing a year of his career at such a crucial time in his development set him back. What made his rehabilitation more difficult was that he had been left behind by those he had grown up with. It wasn't until August 1995 that he got his chance to play in the first team, appearing as a late substitute in a 2–1 win over West Ham.

Although Ferguson had decided to give many of the Class of 92 their opportunity in 1995–96, Thornley still had some catching up to do and in November he was loaned out to Stockport County, making ten appearances for them. Later in the season, he went to Huddersfield Town in Division One, playing 12 games for the Yorkshire outfit. The regular first-team action was an important part in the task of building him up again, and it helped earn him three England Under-21 caps over the summer. But the following campaign, he played only four games for United. He doubled that tally in 1997–98, but all of his Premier League outings came as substitute. With Jesper Blomqvist signed during the summer of 1998, it was clear that he needed to move on if he was to regain some momentum in his career. When he discussed the matter with the boss, Ferguson understood his reasoning and wrote him a letter he has kept to this day, wishing him all the best for the future.

Thornley was given a free transfer and moved back to Huddersfield, signed by Peter Jackson. After a year at the club, his former team-mate Steve Bruce took charge. After he left the Terriers, they were relegated in May 2001 and Thornley moved to Aberdeen. In December 2002, he moved south again, joining Blackpool, but was released at the end of the season. His next stop was at Bury, but it didn't work out for him there. After 171 league appearances, with 11 goals to his credit, he went to non-league Halifax Town (Eric Harrison's former club) and saw out the 2003–04 campaign with them. He eventually finished his career at Witton Albion in Northwich.

Although this was the final postscript to his playing career, it did also provide Thornley with a special moment that he treasures: he spent the season playing with his brother Rod. The latter had always been a very good non-league player, once scoring the goal that sent Altrincham into the Conference. Rod now works as a masseur at United and for England. Meanwhile, Ben has taken up various careers since hanging up his boots, including a period as manager not of a football club but of a Chinese restaurant. He also broadcasts on BBC GMR and MUTV, and still turns out for 'United legends' teams on occasion.

The last one of this group from the Class of 92 to leave United was Chris Casper. Having made his debut in 1994–95, he went on to make his England Under-21 debut after the season finished, lining up alongside Beckham and Phil Neville in a 2–0 win in Toulon over Malaysia. However, he did not play again for United the following campaign. Instead, he was loaned out to Second Division Bournemouth in January 1996. On his debut for Mel Machin's side, who should he line up alongside but George Ndah, who was coming to the end of his loan spell at the club. More than three years on from the FA Youth Cup final, the two former adversaries were now on the same side. To complete the symmetry, both men scored that day – for Casper it was one of only two senior goals in his entire career – and the game turned out to be a fantastic 5–4 thriller.

Casper recalls that he may just have mentioned the Youth Cup final 'once or twice' to Ndah when they were teammates, and earned some good-natured banter in return for his trip down memory lane.

Back at Old Trafford the following campaign with a good deal more senior experience behind him, Casper made six appearances for the Reds, the last of them in a 1–1 draw against Wimbledon in the fourth round of the FA Cup on 25 January 1997 that ended with both sides scoring in the last couple of minutes. He did not realise it then, but it was his seventh and final senior game for United. The following season, he was loaned out again, this time to Swindon Town (by coincidence, he would leave just before Ndah joined them, also on loan). This time he had to wait until his second game for the club to score, but his goal secured all three points and put the club in second place in the First Division. They were still in runners-up spot when he left at the end of October, but Swindon slumped soon after his departure.

With the arrival of Jaap Stam at the start of the 1998–99 season, United's defensive options became even stronger. Having shown what an impact he could have at a lower level, it was not surprising that Second Division Reading should take him, initially on loan. At the age of 23, after more than seven years at United, he says, 'I needed to play first-team football. It was a wrench.' He knew nowhere else would compare. On 4 November, they agreed to pay a fee of £300,000 for the defender, and his presence again seemed to have a beneficial impact on the Royals' form. But on Boxing Day 1999, his left leg was broken in two places by a tackle from Richard Carpenter, and the injury ended his promising career after just 74 league appearances in total. He subsequently won an out-of-court settlement for compensation, but it took six years for it to be sorted.

Of that horrible day, he says, 'You do think about it every day … It changed my life. That said, I don't want tackles going out of the game, but it will stay with me forever.' Carpenter did come to see him in hospital, but Casper was sedated at the time. Even now, in cold or damp conditions, he can still be troubled by the injury.

It was while trying to recover from the injury that he first began to get involved in coaching at the University of Bath. When his leg had sufficiently recovered, he tried to make a comeback, but the pain was too great and he feared a repetition of the injury could have even more severe consequences. Eventually he moved back up north, to Bury, to continue coaching. It was a club he knew well, as his father had been first-team coach there in the 1980s.

He rose through the ranks at Gigg Lane: having started as youth coach, he was eventually appointed manager of the club in October 2005 at just 30 years of age. In his first season, he took over when the club was fighting to avoid relegation to the Conference, and had major financial worries. In his first meeting with the board after taking charge, they told him he had to cut the wage bill while still keeping the club in the Football League. It gave him a chance to blood young players, and they finished in 19th place, losing just one game in their last ten league fixtures, helped by Kasper Schmeichel's good form in goal. He remembers that he spoke often to Eric Harrison to ask his advice, especially as his former manager had started his career at a similar level of the game and so could provide some helpful insights.

Sadly, there was little improvement the following season. Though at one stage Bury were as high as ninth, as the season wore on their form declined. When things failed to pick up the following campaign, Casper lost his job on 14 January 2008, two days after a disappointing 3–0 defeat at Darlington and a run of poor results.

Subsequently, he worked at Bradford City and Grimsby Town before taking on a role with the Premier League in July 2010 as a club support manager. The role involved liaising with all the Premier League clubs in the Northwest, working with their academies and putting in place educational pro-grammes. The idea is to change clubs' two-tier junior structure (academies and centres of excellence) into a four-tier set-up. The problem identified by the Premier League is that only a third of players in the top division have come through Academy system, and this compares poorly with Germany (where the figure is 50 per cent) and Spain (70 per cent).

For Casper, it was a return not only to his geographical roots, but also to the area of football he had emerged from almost 20 years before. The only sadness was that his home-town club, Burnley, had not been able to extend their stay in the top flight so he could have worked there too, just as his father had done. It was also a return to the age group of football where he had first made his name. Who better than a member of the Class of 92 to help show clubs just what potential can be created by a great youth set-up?

So while one member of the Class of 92 set off on a path that would eventually take him back to where he had begun, for the remaining members of the Youth Cup-winning side still at Old Trafford at the start of 1998–99 things were about to take a dramatic turn. It was a story none of them would have dared to dream when they first started as United apprentices back in July 1991.

11

Treble Top and Beyond

'We never gave up. The time to give up is when you're dead.'

Alex Ferguson

If ever a group of kids coming up through the ranks could be said to have transformed a club, then surely the Class of 92 at Manchester United was that group. Although one of their number – Ryan Giggs – had already had a significant impact at United by the summer of 1995, winning the first two of his Premier League titles in 1993 and 1994, as well as other honours, we have seen that the rest of the Youth Cup side were still very much making their way through the ranks. Only Gary Neville (16) and Nicky Butt (11) had started more than ten Premier League games in 1994–95, though the influence of the youngsters grew steadily during the season. Both Butt and Neville took full advantage of the absence of senior players to press their claims for a regular starting place.

However, the established order still ruled at United, with the likes of Bruce, Giggs, Hughes, Ince, Irwin, Kanchelskis, Keane, McClair, Pallister, Schmeichel and Sharpe making the most appearances that campaign. Cantona would have been among their number had it not been for his moment of madness at Selhurst Park, while new signing Andrew Cole had swiftly settled in at Old Trafford.

Alex Ferguson has never been one to let things coast along, and that season – shorn of Cantona for more than three months – United had fallen just short of winning a second successive Double, missing out on the title by a point to Blackburn Rovers and losing the FA Cup final to Everton by a solitary goal. For some, the absence of the talismanic Frenchman might have been sufficient explanation for the shortfall, leading to a belief that his imminent return would soon see normal service resumed. But Ferguson understood that if you let things drift on, then eventually others will overtake you. And for him that has never been an option.

Furthermore, he had seen how well the youngsters had seized their chances since he had begun to blend them into the team; they had shown they could cope with top-level football. One of the Class of 92 – Keith Gillespie – had already been sold on, to Newcastle United as part of the Cole transfer deal. Ferguson didn't want his young stars to get itchy feet because they felt the way forward seemed to be blocked. He was also aware of the old adage put forward by his predecessor, Sir Matt Busby, that most sides have a natural lifespan of about five years before they begin to go off the boil. Many of the 1994–95 side had been together for about that long. Maybe it was time to shake things up a little.

So, during the summer, Ferguson sold Mark Hughes to Chelsea, Paul Ince to Inter Milan and Andrei Kanchelskis to Everton. Three of United's biggest stars had gone, and he brought in no one to replace them. While the departure of Hughes might have been understandable – he was 31 at the time, and it was unlikely that the club would get as good an offer again for the Welshman, who was sold for £1.5 million – the other two were at the peak of their careers. At the time, many of the club's fans were shocked and wondered if the manager had done the right thing.

However, Ferguson wasn't the only one to have been impressed by what he had seen of the United youngsters, and to believe he was right to place his trust in them. England coach Terry Venables gave a debut cap to Gary Neville on 3 June 1995 in a friendly against Japan at Wembley. The following week, he was back in the side to take on Brazil – challenges don't come much bigger than that for a young defender. As the new season got under way, Neville found himself England's first-choice right-back.

United's Premier League campaign began with a trip to Villa Park to take on a team who had finished 18th the previous campaign, one place above the relegation spots. For various reasons, that day United were missing Bruce, Cantona, Cole and Giggs, so the side featured Gary Neville in defence, Butt in midfield and Paul Scholes up front; two others from the Class of 92 – David Beckham and John O'Kane – came off the bench, while Phil Neville, who was even younger than the rest, also started the game in midfield.

Although Beckham scored his first Premier League goal (a stunning strike from 30 yards out that showed just what he was capable of), the six home-grown youngsters could not prevent United from slipping to a disappointing 3–1 defeat. *Match of the Day* pundit Alan Hansen that evening made the comments he is still to live down, pointing out: 'You can't win anything with kids.' He went on to say that for any opposition players looking at the team-sheet: 'It's just going to give them a lift.' He concluded by stating that, even when the four missing players returned, United still did not have enough strength in depth and so he felt it was essential Ferguson bought more players if the club was going to challenge for honours that season.

Ferguson's response over the next couple of games was to introduce first Ben Thornley, then Simon Davies and the returning Giggs to the side – three more products of United's youth system. He was rewarded with two wins, as the Reds began a run where they would drop just four points in ten games. Ferguson had complete confidence in his young players, commenting that in Butt and Roy Keane he had the best central midfield partnership in the Premier League. At the time he said it, it seemed a bold boast, but as the season progressed it became clear that it was merely a statement of fact. He wasn't worried about bringing in 'Fergie's Fledglings', because he had been watching these players develop for years and had seen that they had the temperament to cope with whatever confronted them. His newcomers joined the first team already fully conversant with the United way of doing things.

Treble Top and Beyond

Gary Pallister has recalled a story from their early days in the first team when Butt and Scholes were up against the combative Dennis Wise in the Chelsea midfield. He remembers how they 'stood up for themselves, and gave plenty back with added interest'. It showed they had the character and the courage to compete with anyone, and that they were not going to be intimidated.

Once Cantona returned from his ban at the start of October, bringing his inspirational qualities to the side, United set about reeling in early pace-setters Newcastle United. The Magpies, managed by Kevin Keegan and inspired by Peter Beardsley, Les Ferdinand, David Ginola and Rob Lee, were a formidable outfit. But as the pressure mounted, it began to tell on the experienced side from the Northeast, and not on the young Reds. In what many saw as the decisive game in the title race, United went to St James' Park, where Butt, Giggs and the Neville brothers helped the Manchester side to a 1–0 victory, Phil Neville crossing early in the second half for Cantona to score.

Soon Manchester United were ahead in the race and once they got in front, they were never pegged back. Meanwhile, the Reds had embarked on another cup run, reaching the FA Cup final for the third successive season. Starting with just five of the players who had appeared at Wembley the year before, Beckham, Butt, Giggs, the Neville brothers and Scholes all played a part in United's 1–0 win over Liverpool that secured the double Double, following on from the 1994 success. Between them, those six graduates of United's youth system would go on to make over 3,300 appearances for the club, with the four who played in the 1992 final responsible for almost 2,300 of that total.

While the 1994–95 season was the high-water mark for the Class of 92 in one sense, because nine of those who had played in the Youth Cup campaign turned out for the first team, it was in the following two campaigns when their influence was arguably at its maximum. In both 1995–96 and 1996–97, eight of the Youth Cup squad made at least one appearance for United and in total the Youth Cup team turned out on more than 180 occasions.

Increasingly, the 'kids' were coming of age and were now central to whatever United did; no longer was the focus simply on Cantona. The changeover was symbolised in stunning fashion at the start of the 1996–97 league campaign when Beckham, still just inside his own half, spotted Wimbledon keeper Neil Sullivan slightly off his line. His shot was audacious in its ambition and perfect in its execution as it sailed over the head of the stranded custodian and into the back of the net. Many years later, Sullivan commented on that moment: 'As it left his foot, I thought: "I'm not getting that."'

By that stage, England had a new manager in Glenn Hoddle, and Phil Neville had followed his brother to become an England international, playing in one of the warm-up games to Euro 96, against China in Beijing, alongside his brother. Beckham's goal caught Hoddle's eye and he made his debut in England's first game after the European Championship, against Moldova – one pass-master admiring the work of another. Before the 1996–97 season was over, Butt had joined his three team-mates to become an England international, coming on as a substitute in a March friendly against Mexico. Finally, on 24 May 1997, when England took on

South Africa at Old Trafford, Scholes became the last of the group to earn an England call-up, and four of the United youngsters were on show that day.

Once United had overhauled Liverpool in the title race at the beginning of February 1997, they set a relentless pace and eventually finished seven points clear of runners-up Newcastle. The graduates of the club's youth system knew each other's game inside out. On the right flank, the combination of Beckham and Gary Neville knitted together perfectly. So good were they in tandem, they were soon to become England's regular pairing there, too. It was little surprise when Beckham was awarded the prize as PFA Young Footballer of the Year. Meanwhile, in the centre, while Butt anchored the midfield, Scholes was becoming increasingly influential, whether he was played in midfield or off the main striker. On the left, Giggs continued to give opposition full-backs plenty to think about, with his pace, trickery and skill.

When Cantona retired after the 1996–97 season, the home-grown players took on the mantle of becoming the personification of United. This time, they would fall just short, as Arsenal pipped them to the Premier League title. But they would make up for that in the most stunning way possible in 1998–99.

Although Ferguson had spent a lot of money during the 1998 summer break to provide additional strength in areas where the Class of 92 had not delivered quite as much talent – at the centre of defence and in attack – it was events in France that provided one of the biggest footballing news stories. When Beckham was sent off in the World Cup tie against Argentina, many felt he had cost his country the chance of progressing and he became Public Enemy Number One. His relationship with Victoria Adams, 'Posh Spice' from the Spice Girls, gave his critics another stick with which to beat him. Wherever United travelled that season, Beckham and his family were subjected to the most horrendous abuse. But as far as United fans were concerned, he was their player and he clearly gave his all for the red shirt. That was all that mattered; they gathered round to protect their player and helped inspire him to arguably his finest campaign. The more rival fans jeered him, the more the Red Army backed him.

By now, only four of the 1992 Youth Cup final side were left at the club – Beckham, Butt, Giggs and Gary Neville – while Scholes and Phil Neville from the 1993 side were increasingly important cogs in the United effort. This was the season they truly became an unstoppable machine: after losing 3–2 to Middlesbrough at Old Trafford on 19 December 1998, the Reds did not suffer another defeat before the end of the season as they went in search of a truly astonishing and still unique Treble of Premier League, FA Cup and Champions League trophies. All six men were among those who played more than 40 games for United in the campaign.

They were all in action for what many believe to have been the most dramatic match of the lot, in a season that would have more than its share of thrills and epic encounters. On 14 April, just three days after a 0–0 draw in the first FA Cup semi-final tie, United took on title rivals Arsenal in the replay at Villa Park. All six youth-team graduates played their part in the fixture, and all were on the pitch at the end. According to Gary Neville, it was 'quite simply the best [game] I've ever played in'.

United took the lead after 17 minutes when Beckham curled one from just outside the penalty area past his England team-mate David Seaman. But United couldn't find a second goal that would put the tie firmly in their favour, and midway through the second half Dennis Bergkamp equalised. Soon after, Keane was sent off, and then, on the verge of full time, Arsenal were awarded a penalty after a Phil Neville foul. The Treble dream was surely over – but Peter Schmeichel saved it. In extra time, United seemed to be hanging on in the hope of taking the game to a penalty shoot-out, until a misplaced pass from Patrick Vieira set Giggs free in space, and he went on a run from just inside his own half.

A few days before, the Welshman had been reminded by Ferguson that his 'pace and direct running at defenders' were his key assets. Having come on for Jesper Blomqvist after an hour, Giggs still had the energy to run at the Gunners defence and then to blast the ball past the helpless Seaman to score one of the greatest – and most important – goals in the club's recent history. As Giggs has commented, it was 'my best goal ever, and the one I'd like to be remembered by'.

There were just over ten minutes left, and the ten men of United hung on for a famous victory. The pitch invasion that followed the final whistle showed just what the result had meant to everyone who supported the Reds. The manager revealed the attitude that had brought about such a stunning result: 'We never gave up. The time to give up is when you're dead.'

A week later, United went to the Stadio delle Alpi to take on Juventus in the second leg of the Champions League semi-final. Having struggled against the Italians at Old

Trafford, where a very late Giggs equaliser saved the day, the Reds knew they would probably have to win in Italy for the first time in their history to qualify for the final. So going 2–0 down in the first ten minutes was definitely not part of the plan. The game is usually remembered as Keane's match, for the inspirational performance put in by United's captain, especially given the fact that when he picked up a booking he knew he would not be taking part in the final if his side got there.

Keane pulled back the first goal from a Beckham corner, before Dwight Yorke and then Cole scored the goals that put United through. Giggs had missed this comeback through an injury picked up in the Arsenal game, but another member of the Class of 92 knew he was also going to miss the final. Scholes was booked for a foul on Didier Deschamps that meant he too was banned from playing in the biggest match of his career to date.

With two finals to look forward to, United could focus on the title race. The Reds led by a point from Arsenal and had a game in hand, but United's draw the following weekend at Leeds United gave the Gunners a slight edge. When United then let slip a 2–0 lead at Anfield on 5 May, finishing with a 2–2 draw, they were three points behind Arsenal, but a win at Middlesbrough put them top on goal difference. Arsenal then lost at Leeds and the Reds drew at Blackburn, which meant on the final day United, now leading by a point, would win the league if their result against Spurs at least matched Arsenal's against Aston Villa.

Les Ferdinand, who had been part of the Newcastle side that had suffered at United's hands in 1996, scored first for

Tottenham at Old Trafford to leave the title heading for Highbury. Then, just before half time, Scholes passed to Beckham inside the box and he scored the equaliser that gave the advantage back to United. Early in the second period, from just inside the Spurs half, Gary Neville lifted a left-foot pass into the box, where Cole brought it under control and lobbed home a fine finish to give the Reds the lead. Even though Arsenal subsequently took the lead in their game, it wasn't enough to stop United from taking the title. And, as with the FA Cup semi-final, all six former youth-teamers played their part in the victory.

With one title won, next up was the FA Cup final against Newcastle United. Given the absence of Keane and Scholes from central midfield for the forthcoming Champions League final, it was deemed too risky to play Butt in this game, so he was rested, but the other five graduates of the Class of 92 all played. After the previous dramas, this game never reached the heights that so many others had done.

After 11 minutes, Scholes opened up the Newcastle defence with a superb pass to Teddy Sheringham, who slotted it past Steve Harper in the Magpies goal. Early in the second half, Sheringham returned the favour, laying the ball back for Scholes to rifle home with his left foot from 20 yards. United were playing with such confidence that at one stage Gary Neville even dummied Alan Shearer before clearing the ball. The 2–0 win secured United's third Double in five years, but there was still one more game to go.

With Scholes banned and Phil Neville on the bench, it was United's four surviving members of the Class of 92 who took the field in Barcelona's Nou Camp Stadium on 26 May 1999 to meet Bayern Munich in the Champions League final. Beckham and Butt were paired together in the centre of midfield, while Giggs was moved across to the right to accommodate Blomqvist on the left; Gary Neville was of course at right-back.

As part of his speech to the players, Ferguson had warned them against the agony of having to walk past the trophy at the end of the game and not be able to touch it. For most of the game, it looked as though their worst fears were going to be realised. The Germans took the lead after just six minutes, and subsequently hit the woodwork twice as the Reds struggled to maintain any sort of grip on their opponents.

However, many of these players had grown up together and they trusted each other. As Ferguson had said before, they would never give up. That was why, just as the fourth official held up the board to say there would be three minutes of added time, Gary Neville dashed across the pitch to take a throw-in on United's left side, down by the Bayern corner flag. He recalled: 'It's what I'd been taught to do since I was a kid at United. You keep playing, you keep trying, you keep sprinting until the death.' From that throw-in, United won a corner.

Beckham rushed over to take it, but it was half-cleared and the ball fell to Giggs on the edge of the box. He didn't quite catch his right-foot volley truly, but as it headed towards goal, Sheringham deflected it past Oliver Kahn and into the goal. United weren't done. In the third minute of added time, they got another corner out on the left. Again Beckham swung it in; Sheringham, on the edge of the six-yard box, flicked it on; and Ole Gunnar Solskjaer stuck out a foot to volley it into the top of the net. Cue pandemonium!

With Sir Bobby Charlton (himself a former United Youth Cup winner in 1954, 1955 and 1956 as well as a European Cup winner in 1968) looking on from the stands, the players and the fans went wild with delight, as United secured their second title as European champions. The Class of 92 were at the heart of it. In his memoirs, Beckham recalled how special those moments he shared with the fans were: 'If it hadn't been for the supporters [backing him after the World Cup] ... I'm not sure I'd have been there.'

To give some idea of how unusual an achievement this was – to have four players from the same youth team lining up in the biggest club game of them all – compare the situation a decade later. In 2008, United were again the winners of the Champions League, and their victory came just five years after the club had won the Youth Cup back in 2003. From that 2003 side, only Chris Eagles (with six) and Phil Bardsley (one) made any appearances at all for United in 2007–08. Even back in the 1960s, when player transfers were less frequent than they are in more modern times and when overseas players were almost unheard of in the British game, the Youth Cup-winning side of 1964 still provided only three players – John Aston, George Best and David Sadler – for United's 1968 European Cup final team. In fact, outside of United, only Jamie Carragher of Liverpool has managed to win both the Youth Cup and pick up a Champions League winner's medal for the same club, while all three of United's European champion sides have featured players who won the Youth Cup with the club.

After that incredible high, when the Reds won the lot, there was only ever going to be one way to go – especially when the FA insisted United go to Brazil for the Club World Championship in January 2000, which meant they could not even defend one of their trophies. However, the league title was still won by a stunning margin of 18 points, and featured a moment of special genius between two of the Class of 92. It came on 25 March away to Bradford City. Beckham took a corner from the left and it came to Scholes at a perfect height, 20 yards out, level with the right-hand goalpost. Scholes volleyed it first time into the corner of the net – an unstoppable shot that showed not only incredible technique and skill from both men, but also an almost telepathic mutual understanding that had been developed over a decade playing together.

Then, in 2000–01, United completed a hat-trick of Premier League titles, this time by a margin of ten points – but it was only that close because they lost the last three games after they had already wrapped up the league. The Reds seemed almost scarily dominant in England, with Arsenal often their only realistic challengers.

But in 2001–02 there was a fall-off in performance as United finished in third position, ten points behind champions Arsenal. The chance of another Champions League final was missed when the Reds lost out to Bayer Leverkusen in the semi-finals on the away goals rule. United bounced back the following season to win their eighth Premier League title, but 11 years after that famous win in the Youth Cup of 1992, Sir Alex decided that the time had come to begin to move things on – he wanted to avoid having the situation where a large number of the side began to age at the same time. Just as it had been in 1995, when he'd let go so many key figures, the ploy was a controversial one, but his justification came with the results that followed.

The first to go, in the summer of 2003, was David Beckham, sold to Real Madrid for about £25 million. By now the world's most famous footballer, some in the media had begun to question whether his off-the-pitch activities were distracting him from the day job. However, there is no doubt that his love for United and commitment to the cause, carried forward from his boyhood days, remained as strong as ever. Although just 28 at the time, Beckham had made 394 appearances in the United shirt, scoring 85 goals. He had also been England captain since November 2000.

At Madrid, he initially linked up with former United assistant manager Carlos Queiroz. Playing alongside fellow *galacticos* Zinedine Zidane and Luís Figo in the midfield, and with a star-studded squad that also included Brazilians Ronaldo and Roberto Carlos, as well as Raúl, Beckham was seen as the jewel in this starriest of crowns. But despite all the talent on display, they won nothing that year and Queiroz was gone. The next two seasons were turbulent ones in the Madrid boardroom and in the manager's seat, which did not help the club on the field.

With Beckham still trophyless at Madrid after three seasons at the club, in 2006–07 Fabio Capello took charge. The strict Italian was wary of the cult of celebrity that wrapped itself around too many of the Madrid side, and initially Beckham was one to suffer. Midway through the season it was announced that his contract would not be renewed, after which he decided to move to LA Galaxy. Capello said the Londoner would not play for the side again, but Beckham continued to work hard in training and forced the manager to change his mind. He was rewarded with some fine performances by the former United man, and the club ended the season by winning La Liga.

Some felt that Beckham's highly lucrative move to the USA signalled the end of his career at international level, but the man himself had not given up on his England career. He had stepped down as England captain after the 2006 World Cup, but had not expected Sven-Göran Eriksson's successor Steve McClaren would thereafter drop him from the side, especially as the two had worked together at United. His form in the second half of the season at Madrid earned him an England recall in May 2007. It had proved impossible for McClaren to ignore his dedication.

Once Beckham went to Los Angeles, he had a series of injuries that suggested he might be left stranded on 99 caps, especially when Capello took charge of the England side after the 2008 European Championships. The lure of the Hollywood lifestyle (he became friends with Tom Cruise, among others), not to mention a wide range of Beckham-branded products, was surely going to be too much of a distraction. Again, Beckham's commitment never wavered, and he had two loan spells at Milan in 2008–09 and 2009–10 to show he was still capable of playing at the highest level of club football.

During his second Italian stay, Beckham was part of the side that took on United in the Champions League round of 16. Milan were outclassed in both legs, but on his first senior appearance back at Old Trafford he was given a huge ovation by the United faithful when he came on as a second-half substitute (and well-meaning boos every time he touched the ball); he very nearly even scored a spectacular consolation goal. Eventually, Beckham finished his England career with 115 caps – overhauling Bobby Moore's record for an outfield player – and in November 2011 he won the MLS title with LA Galaxy. After five years at the club, it was announced early in 2012 that he would play for them for another two seasons.

After Beckham's departure, United also failed to win the league. Arsenal's 'Invincibles' managed to go through the entire 2003–04 Premier League season unbeaten. Sir Alex Ferguson responded by continuing to ring the changes as far as the Class of 92 was concerned, and Nicky Butt was sold to Newcastle United for £2.5 million while the club were on their summer tour of the USA. In his final two seasons at United, he had fallen behind Keane and Scholes as part of United's regular central midfield pairing. With Darren Fletcher becoming an increasingly frequent starter, it was clear the manager was once again turning to youth to build another great side.

For Butt, the move to the Magpies seemed a good one. Under Sir Bobby Robson, they had finished in the top five for the previous three seasons, and for Butt there was the lure of more European football. But, to widespread astonishment, Robson was sacked just four games into the new campaign, and Graeme Souness took charge. Butt had some niggling injuries that season, and so found himself in and out of the side, unable to get a regular place in the line-up. Some of the Geordie fans, comparing his performances with what they had seen from him at United, thought he was coasting and taking advantage of the club. When the Reds knocked

Newcastle out of the FA Cup in the semi-finals, rumours swept around that he was seen laughing with Sir Alex after the game and that he had travelled back to Manchester rather than with his team-mates. It wasn't true, though Butt admitted he could understand the fans' frustrations when the stories circulated.

In the summer of 2005, Souness bought Scott Parker and Belözoğlu Emre to strengthen his midfield options, telling Butt that he would be part of the squad. It wasn't what he wanted – as he pointed out at the time, he would have stayed at Old Trafford if he had been content to be a squad player. So Butt joined Steve Bruce at Birmingham City for a season on loan with the Blues. Having known the former Reds captain since he was 14, he felt it would give him an opportunity to enjoy his football again after a couple of frustrating seasons. His spell at St Andrews did the trick, and he returned to the Northeast, where Glenn Roeder was now in charge. For the next three seasons, he played in more than 30 Premier League games in each campaign, something he had not managed since the 1990s. But at the end of 2008–09 (by which stage there had been four more managers employed at the club), the Magpies were relegated. In 2009–10, for the first time in his career at the age of 34, Butt was playing outside the Premier League.

Now club captain, Butt featured in only 17 league games all season, and decided to announce his retirement just before the end of the campaign, as Chris Hughton's side celebrated promotion back to the top flight. It wasn't quite the end, however, as he played a few games the following season for South China.

As well as having played some 411 Premier League games (fewer than 20 players have appeared more often in the competition), scoring 29 goals, Butt also won 39 England caps. He was arguably at his peak for England in the 2002 World Cup, when Pelé picked him out as the one in the England side that the Brazilians most feared. Butt's response to this endorsement was typical of the man: 'There were a lot better players than me at that World Cup. I know that, everyone knows that.' He was always keen to avoid the limelight and be allowed simply to get on with the job in hand.

Having returned to Old Trafford to play in testimonial matches for Gary Neville and Scholes, Butt soon found himself back at Carrington in 2011–12. This time, he was there to work on his coaching badges, watch how the sessions were conducted and learn from the staff. He noted: 'Ask any player and the knowledge is in their head. The difficult part is getting the point across and doing it clearly. That is what I've got to learn.' But he was clear about his ambition to develop into a manager. One suspects that if he does, he will make a formidable foe, and one who will never let his players get carried away with what they have achieved. After all he has won, his feet are still very firmly on the ground – and woe betide anyone who is ever satisfied or believes they can drift along in their comfort zone.

By the start of the 2004–05 season, the combination of Roman Abramovich's billions and José Mourinho's management skills had created a new major rival for United in Chelsea. The Blues went on to win the title that year by a massive margin, with United 18 points behind them in third – it remains the club's worst performance, relative to the title winners, in the Premier League era.

Ferguson continued his policy of trying to lower the average age of his squad. At the end of the campaign another long-serving graduate of the youth system, Phil Neville, was allowed to leave. He had made 386 appearances for United, scoring eight goals in total. He was sold to Everton for around £3.5 million on 4 August 2005. Like Butt before him, he had spent his final season at United as an irregular first choice, partly because he was one of the most adaptable players in the squad, capable of playing in either full-back role or a holding role in the midfield. At the time, Neville commented: 'This has been the most difficult decision I have ever had to make.'

It wasn't just a case of his sadness at leaving United, but there was the knowledge that 'the Manc' (as he is known by his Toffees team-mates) would have to prove that his heart was really with his new employers, or whether it remained back down the M62 in Manchester. However, he'd heard Everton might be interested in taking him on before the summer break and the idea of a fresh start began to appeal to him. Ferguson had a long meeting with him to discuss his options, both at United (where he would have happily retained him) and elsewhere. It was handled in such a way that Neville subsequently commented: 'It was more like a father speaking.'

Those who had their doubts about Neville's commitment to his new cause did not know their man. Toffees manager David Moyes was absolutely sure what he was getting: he knew Neville was a 'professional's professional'. With a

European campaign in the offing, having finished fourth the previous season, Everton were keen to have his experience in their line-up – he had played 64 Champions League games for United.

While Neville was unable to help Everton to any success in Europe, the 28-year-old did bring to the Merseyside outfit a new level of dedication and professionalism that had Moyes appointing him club captain the following season. In fact, he was first handed the armband within a few weeks of joining Everton, and Neville was aware this might upset people. He responded by trying to set a professional example to all around him. Soon, the things he did in training – such as starting early – were being done by others. It echoed his brother's recollections of when he signed up as an apprentice and was called 'Busy' for always doing a little bit more than he had to. It was just what Moyes had been looking for.

Phil Neville's first game back at Old Trafford was a strange one. Trying to focus on the game, and to show his team-mates that he was not being too familiar with the opposition, he felt the tension was rising. 'Then Scholesy shouted "smile" and after that I couldn't stop laughing,' he recalls. The game ended 1–1, but also featured newly appointed United captain Gary kicking the ball at his brother during a stoppage: business first; family second.

The following season, on 29 November 2006, Premier League history was made when the two Neville brothers lined up against each other as captains of their side. Gary and United emerged from that contest as 3–0 winners. In his first four seasons at Goodison Park, Phil Neville missed just nine games in total. Moyes may have an impressive track record in the transfer market, but it is hard to think he will have made many more worthwhile signings in his career.

By Easter in the 2011–12 season, Neville had made 220 Premier League appearances for his new club, on top of the 263 at United. That total of 483 put him in the all-time top ten appearance-makers in the competition, and there is every chance he will become the seventh player to top 500 games in the Premier League. Now 35, he continues to go about his job quietly and efficiently, the model professional. He won his 59th and last England cap in 2007, and while he was in the squad for three European Championships he was never selected for England in a World Cup tournament.

So, with Beckham, Butt and Phil Neville gone and United temporarily off the pace in the league, there were now just three members of the Class of 92 left at the club as Ferguson prepared for the 2005–06 season. Giggs, Gary Neville and Scholes had all turned 30; 'Fergie's Fledglings' had grown up. Could they help a new generation of United players take the club back to the summit? Could the pupils from the Class of 92 now become the teachers?

12

The Master Class of 92

'It doesn't get any better than that. It's a feeling that won't change whether you're seventeen or thirty-eight.'

Ryan Giggs, after scoring a last-minute winner

As the 2005–06 season began, many pundits were questioning whether United's long period of dominance had come to an end. Had the beating heart of United gone? When the Reds came last in their Champions League group, scoring only three goals in six games, some felt they had their answer. The sudden departure of Roy Keane, after 12 years at the club, was seen by some as further evidence that the wheels were coming off. But Sir Alex Ferguson was confident he was building a new team that could match anything achieved by their predecessors. This time, his team would be a compelling blend of youth and experience, with the youth supplied by the likes of Cristiano Ronaldo and Wayne Rooney. The experience came from the old guard who had been at the club for more than a decade and had seen it all before.

After a difficult first few months, that campaign did have its trophy-winning consolation with victory in the Carling Cup, a 4–0 stroll against Wigan at Cardiff's Millennium Stadium. Some critics commented that this was small compensation for a club of United's stature, where success was usually measured only in Premier League titles and Champions League finals. But the members of the Class of 92 knew differently.

Gary Neville, who had taken over as club captain after the departure of Keane, was thrilled to have won his first trophy as skipper. Afterwards he commented: 'It is obvious to everyone that this team is growing. It's gone through some transition over the last couple of years. The people who watch the club know that we are going in the right direction.'

Giggs echoed his thoughts: '[The League Cup] was the first trophy I ever won and it gives you a taste of success. It lets you know what United is all about: winning trophies, doing the lap of honour, having a medal. This is the first trophy for many of the players, so hopefully it can do what it did for me and give them a taste for success that makes you want more.'

Among those newcomers who were picking up their first major trophies at United were experienced Dutch goalkeeper Edwin van der Sar, Patrice Evra and Nemanja Vidić in defence, Kieran Richardson and Ji-Sung Park in midfield, and Rooney and Louis Saha in attack. As Giggs had hoped, they did pick up the taste very quickly, for the following season United were back on top of the table, beating Chelsea to the title by six points, having led from the front from the beginning of October. Where others had wilted in the face of Chelsea's billionaire challenge, United had simply upped their game again.

By this stage, Giggs, Neville and Scholes were all either 32 or 33 years old, and Sir Alex was beginning to manage their time on the pitch to preserve their influence on events. The habit of squad rotation he had introduced to give them their chance as teenagers was now being used to prolong their careers. However, when Neville picked up an ankle ligament injury against Bolton Wanderers in March 2007, it had a major impact on the rest of his career. Having been an England regular for more than a decade, he would never again play for his country after winning 85 caps.

Because of his injury problems, Neville missed almost the entire 2007–08 season, so it was left to Giggs and Scholes to fly the flag for the Class of 92. As the campaign moved towards 'squeaky bum time' in spring, there was talk of another Champions League triumph while they battled with Arsenal and Chelsea for the Premier League title. Giggs and Scholes continued to be the age-defying pulse of the team, providing the creative input for United's four-pronged strike force of Ronaldo, Rooney, Saha and Carlos Tévez. The two veterans were no longer quite the same goal threat they had been in earlier years, but instead their vision for a telling pass seemed to improve with age.

The route to the Champions League final was barred by Barcelona in the semi-finals. Against a side featuring the talents of Xavi Hernández, Andrés Iniesta and Lionel Messi, not to mention Samuel Eto'o, Yaya Touré and an old foe in Thierry Henry, United held the Catalan side to a 0–0 draw in the Nou Camp in front of almost 96,000 fans. In truth, it was a disappointing game as an attacking spectacle, but a brilliant defensive performance by United to nullify the famed Barça attack. After 14 minutes of the second leg at Old Trafford, a poor clearance from Gianluca Zambrotta fell at the feet of Scholes in space 30 yards out. After taking a touch, he smashed it into the top right-hand corner of the goal, curling away from the despairing dive of Victor Valdés. Roared on by the Old Trafford faithful, the man who had missed out on the 1999 final had taken United back there in 2008. As he has commented: it was 'by far the most important goal I've ever scored'.

In the final itself, Sir Alex was in no doubt that Scholes would start, having been absent nine years earlier. United's opponents were very familiar: Chelsea, the team the Reds had just beaten to the league title again. The final took place in the Luzhniki Stadium in Moscow, so many pundits felt the fates were in favour of Abramovich's club. But Ronaldo gave United the lead, before Frank Lampard equalised just before half time. Thereafter, the game became tense, with more chances falling to the London side. Late on, Giggs came on to the pitch to make his 759th appearance for United – it was the one that took him past Sir Bobby Charlton to become the all-time leading appearance-maker for the club – and he almost scored.

Extra time was necessary, but no further goals were scored, so United faced a penalty shoot-out to see if they could win their third European title. After five penalties each, the scores were level, so it was sudden death. Anderson hit home for United, while Salomon Kalou kept Chelsea in it. Then it was Giggs's turn. Would he ruin his record-breaking night? No. He hit it cleanly into the bottom-right corner, beyond the reach of Petr Cech, and when Nicolas Anelka had his penalty saved by van der Sar, United were European champions again.

Afterwards, Giggs set the tone that reflected the United way of doing things: 'We want to be competing for the Champions League every year. We can kick on, where we didn't last time. The difference between now and 1999 is that this is a young team.'

As Giggs had been used as a late substitute in both legs of the semi-final and in the final itself, not coming on until after 75 minutes had been played in each instance, some wondered if the man who had captained the Youth Cup final side 16 years earlier was thinking of bringing his career to a close. But in 2008–09, he made more appearances than in the previous campaign. With Scholes and the returning Neville, he continued to set the standards and to provide the inspirational example of what playing for United meant.

Having signed Dimitar Berbatov for a club record fee of £30.75 million, United went close to winning the lot. In Japan, the Reds became the first English side to win the Club World Cup; and in March they followed it with the Carling Cup. In April, having fielded a much-changed side, United fell to Everton in a penalty shoot-out in the FA Cup semi-final (former Red Phil Neville scoring one of the penalties). The following month, the Premier League title was back at Old Trafford for the third successive season and the 11th time in all. And after a comprehensive Champions League semi-final victory over Arsenal, United went to Rome to take on Barcelona in the final.

Whereas the previous season Giggs had come on for Scholes in the final, this time it was the other way round, but neither man could turn the tide and the Spanish side ran out comfortable 2–0 winners. It took something of the gloss off what had been another remarkable campaign. But for Giggs there was a personal honour, too, as he was voted the PFA Player of the Year. The lessons he had learned at the very beginning of his United career – never to be satisfied, always to see what more you can do to be better and to win more trophies – were the ones his fellow professionals saw him passing on to his team-mates, helping the new stars of the side to ever greater efforts. He may not have been as vocal as Keane, but the example Giggs set was arguably even more inspirational.

And so it proved in 2009–10 when, following the departure of Ronaldo to Real Madrid, Giggs began taking more free kicks when there was a shooting opportunity. He admitted in interview that, with the departure of the Portuguese star, there was more scope for him to do this and so he had been working on that aspect of his game. He might have hit 36 years of age in November, but he was still looking to offer new skills to the side to make himself as indispensable as possible.

It was to be the final campaign when Giggs, Neville and Scholes all still operated as full participants, but United missed out on a record-breaking fourth successive league title, and had to content themselves with winning just the Carling

Cup. For Neville, who came on as a substitute, it was his last winner's medal at United.

No one realised it at the time, but Saturday 11 September 2010 was a significant landmark. It was the last game when Giggs, Neville and Scholes lined up together for United. At Goodison Park, Gary's brother Phil watched on from the bench in amazement as the Toffees came back from 3–1 down in added time to equalise. It was the sort of comeback that was usually United's speciality.

It was one of just four appearances for Gary Neville that season, as he announced his retirement in mid-campaign. A succession of injuries had left him feeling slightly off the pace, and as someone who had always set high standards for himself and demanded them of others, he was not going to allow himself to slip below them. Early in February 2011, after 602 appearances for United during which time he had picked up eight league winners' medals along with numerous other honours, he decided to retire: 'It just felt like the right thing to do and that my time was up ... You don't want to be a passenger.'

By that stage, Neville may no longer have been club captain, but he had always set a great example to those around him. When he had first joined the club, his father had said to him: 'Gary, make sure you don't look back thinking "I wish I'd done more".' He had followed that piece of advice to the letter. From youth-team coach Eric Harrison he had learned that each training session 'had to be treated like a cup final'. As the Class of 92 grew older, and became the respected elder statesmen of the side, it was these messages that were transmitted to their younger team-mates. While they have been around, the Old Trafford dressing room has never been a place where egos are allowed to run rampant or where words fail to match deeds. In the modern world of mega-salaried footballers, this down-to-earth attitude, learned from Harrison, Ferguson and all the coaching staff, is one thing that has helped to set United apart from their rivals time and time again.

Former team-mate Nicky Butt had always assumed Neville would make a natural manager when his playing career was over. But others noted how he also enjoyed talking (his 'favourite pastime' according to Giggs) – he was renowned as a shop steward figure within both the United and the England dressing rooms. And it was his ability to talk knowledgeably about the game that provided him with his next career move. He had already had a few attempts at television punditry while still a player, but Sky Sports announced they had recruited the United man for a major role at the station in 2011–12.

To United fans, used to hearing former Liverpool players on most stations, the voice of 'Red Nev' was a welcome addition. Very quickly he proved himself a brilliant expert summariser and pundit. His technical analysis provided new insights – such as why defenders should be taught to keep their steps small when closing down someone on the point of shooting (to avoid the possibility of the ball going through their legs). It was also occasionally very funny, as shown by his description of Chelsea's David Luiz as being 'controlled by a ten-year-old in the crowd on a PlayStation'.

As the 2010–11 season wound towards a close, United fans were delighted to hear that Giggs had signed a contract to keep him at Old Trafford for another season, but there was no news on Scholes. The one who hadn't quite made it into the Youth Cup side in 1992 was clearly mulling over whether or not to retire. Fortunately, there was plenty to distract him from making that decision, as United were inevitably on the hunt for a 12th Premier League title, the one that would take the club past Liverpool's overall record of 18 league titles, as United had also been champions seven times before the Premier League era.

The Reds duly picked up their title with a game to spare after a 1–1 draw at Ewood Park against Blackburn Rovers, with both Giggs and Scholes playing their part in the game. Though delighted for his senior players, the manager also focused on the fact that it was a first title for Darron Gibson, Javier Hernández and Chris Smalling. For Giggs, winning his record-extending 12th title, 'Those are the nights you love . . . it's just a great celebration.'

But in the week between the final league game and the Champions League final, there were two more games to savour. First of all, Paul McGuinness's side were in the final of the Youth Cup. After drawing 2–2 with Sheffield United in front of almost 30,000 fans at Bramall Lane on 17 May, six days later the second leg was held at Old Trafford. A crowd of 24,916 saw Ravel Morrison and Will Keane both score twice to give the Reds a 4–1 victory on the night. It was United's record-extending tenth victory in the tournament and showed that the Class of 92 had their loyal imitators in the new generation.

The next day, Gary Neville testimonial saw a reunion of many of the Class of 92 side, including David Beckham,

Butt, Giggs, Phil Neville and Scholes, as United took on Juventus. Within 24 hours of each other, the history of the club and the future were being celebrated.

And it was to history that United looked for omens in the Champions League final, which was held at Wembley, where the club had won its first European title back in 1968. The more recent omen came in the shape of the opposition – Barcelona, who had beaten the Reds so convincingly in 2009 to take the trophy on that occasion. Sadly, it was that part of history that repeated itself, as United lost 3–1, with Giggs and substitute Scholes again unable to swing things in favour of United.

Already, though, Giggs was looking forward: 'It's about pushing into the twenties [of titles]. That's what this club is about: not standing still, but moving forward.' However, for Scholes there was a different decision to make. Having made 676 appearances for United, and scored 150 goals, winning ten league titles in the process, he decided to retire. However, he was not going to be lost to the club: he chose to stay on to help coach the young players coming through. He would keep the focus on the future, while helping to maintain the traditions that had served the club so well.

With veteran keeper Edwin van der Sar also having retired, United started 2011–12 with a new look and at the start of the campaign Sir Alex fielded some of the youngest sides he'd ever put out. During the summer he had recruited 20-year-old goalkeeper David de Gea from Spain, 19-year-old defender Phil Jones from Blackburn Rovers and winger Ashley Young from Aston Villa, while two products of the club's youth system, midfielder Tom Cleverley and striker Danny Welbeck, were brought back from loan spells. They got off to a superb start, with the most remarkable result being an 8–2 thrashing of an injury-hit Arsenal side.

Welbeck spoke about the influence of the Class of 92: 'Obviously it's motivational to see. Sir Alex Ferguson was breeding his group, the Class of Ninety-two, into the first team as well and they did really well. They came through Academy and went all the way, so our coaches were saying to us: "If they can do it, why can't you?" That was the mentality that everybody had, so you just had to use that and work as hard as you could on the training pitch. It made sure that even when you went home, you were still training yourselves, not just making sure you did it when you were at the training ground. It was that love of football and how much you enjoyed it and how hard you worked to succeed.'

As the season wore on, however, United were themselves hit by a number of injuries, depleting their squad and leading to some disappointing results. The defence and central midfield were worst hit, with Michael Carrick and Patrice Evra having to fill in at centre-back, while the heart of the midfield was on one occasion manned by Ji-Sung Park and Rafael. Whatever their various gifts, these were not the combinations the manager would have chosen if he'd had a full squad to pick from.

More than two decades since making his first-team debut, Giggs was still playing his part, and had set yet another record as he became the only man to play (and score) in 20 successive Premier League seasons. Now usually used in the centre of midfield, the Welshman continued to astonish and inspire all around him by his longevity. His new role had given him a new lease of life, and though he admitted that 'I probably feel at my best when I'm playing every ten days or two weeks', he was still able to cope with two games in four days when the need arose. It all left Sir Alex looking on in amazement: 'There has been no discernible deterioration in his play whatsoever.'

On 26 February 2012, Giggs reached the landmark of playing 900 senior games for United. He made sure it was a special day, too. United's trip to Carrow Road was an important one, as in-form Norwich City looked certain to give the Reds a tough game. With league leaders Manchester City having won the day before to open up a five-point gap over United, nothing less than a win would do. Late in the second half, the Canaries scored the equaliser their performance merited, but it served only to galvanise the Reds. With the game into its second minute of added time, Young swung in a cross and who should be on the end of it but Giggs? He steered it home from four yards out and then ran off to celebrate with the travelling supporters. He commented afterwards: 'It doesn't get any better than that. It's a feeling that won't change whether you're seventeen or thirty-eight, like I am now.' The manager stressed another reason why the goal was so important: 'Everyone knows we never give in and no matter who plays us they know they're going to have to play right until the very death.'

Having also won 64 caps for Wales between 16 October 1991 and 2 June 2007 (scoring 12 goals), Giggs's next aim was to top 1000 senior appearances, and with another contract already agreed for 2012–13 that target should be passed before the year is out. By Easter 2012, he had scored 163 goals for the club, putting him joint eighth in the all-time list, level with his former team-mate and fellow Welshman Mark Hughes.

Like the man he was so often compared with early in his career – George Best – Giggs was never able to perform in a major international tournament, as Wales have not qualified for either the World Cup or the European Championship finals since 1958. It is one of the very few gaps in his CV, and rumours persisted throughout the season that he might be recruited to line up for Great Britain in the London Olympics as one of the over-age players. He was appointed an OBE in 2007 and won the BBC Sports Personality of the Year Award in 2009.

Speaking to *Inside United* magazine during the 2011–12 season, Giggs talked about his role as a senior statesman at the club, especially now there were so many young faces in the squad: 'That [responsibility] comes when these young players are either injured, aren't playing, or have lost form. That's when, really, you need to help them ... That's when your experience comes in because we've all been there.' He explained how he knows when to say something: 'It's that next tier from the coaching staff to the dressing room – there are things you see first-hand. It's especially so for me because I don't play every game, so sometimes you're watching games and you see things that can help young players.'

After a few months as the sole survivor of the Class of 92, on 8 January 2012 Sir Alex sprang a surprise on Giggs and the rest of the squad when he gave out the team-sheet. United were preparing to take on 'noisy neighbours' Manchester City in the third round of the FA Cup at the

Etihad Stadium. Listed among the substitutes, and wearing the Number 22 shirt, was his latest recruit: a 37-year-old midfielder named Paul Scholes. Sitting in the City dugout, Brian Kidd, who had worked with Scholes more than 20 years earlier when he was United's youth development officer, must have feared the worst. Having missed half the season, Scholes realised that he had been too hasty in giving up his playing career. He was back for more. With half an hour of the game to go, he came on to help United see the game through to a famous 3–2 victory that set up another mouth-watering cup-tie – at Anfield against Liverpool.

Astonishingly, it was as if he had never been away. He had been training hard with the Reserves while working towards his 'A' coaching licence and was clearly still enjoying his football. As Giggs revealed, the youngsters were telling him that 'he was still the best in training'. The manager said that when Scholes told him he wanted to come back: 'He approached me about it and to me there were no negatives ... He never panics when he's on the ball ... He's a great person to have in the dressing room too. The players genuinely look up to him and Ryan Giggs as their mentors and their teachers.' Giggs agreed that Scholes's return gave everyone a 'massive boost'. The Welshman added: 'He's a one-off ... He'll either sit in front of the back four and dictate the game, or he'll get on the end of crosses and score goals.'

So it proved. In his first start in his second coming, just six days later against Bolton, Scholes was on the end of a Rooney cross to score his 151st goal for United, putting him ahead of Ruud van Nistelrooy at number ten in the Reds' list of top goalscorers. Having retired 12 appearances short of Bill

Foulkes's total of 688, he overhauled the Busby-era defender to move into third spot behind his long-time team-mate Giggs and one of his greatest fans, Sir Bobby Charlton, when he played in United's 5–0 victory at Wolverhampton Wanderers on 18 March 2012, a game that saw the Reds move four points clear at the top of the table.

Within weeks of his return, media speculation began to grow as to whether, with a new England manager in place for the European Championships, he might be persuaded out of international retirement as well this summer. He had made 66 appearances for England between 1997 and 2004, scoring 14 goals. He had retired in August of that year, citing family reasons, but there was also a sense of frustration that Sven-Göran Eriksson had played him out of position on the left side of midfield to accommodate both Steven Gerrard and Frank Lampard in the centre. If anything were to come of it, it would surely be one of the most astonishing football comebacks of all time. It is also a mark of the respect in which he is held throughout the game that few would begrudge him his place.

The Norwich game at the end of February wasn't just the Giggs show, as the scorer of the other goal in that 2–1 win was Scholes. After the game, the manager hailed the two veterans by saying, 'Scholes and Giggs are the best players this club has ever had. That experience is really going to help us in [the title run-in].'

Remarkably, 20 years on, the story of the Class of 92 has not yet reached its final chapter. But it is one that is unlikely ever to be repeated. As we have seen, only rarely do the stars of youth teams go on to have success at the clubs where they grew up. Yet this group of kids went on to play thousands of games at senior level. Giggs and Gary Neville went on to captain United. Butt and Phil Neville, who won everything at Old Trafford, went on to captain other Premier League clubs, as United's rivals tried to replicate the secrets of the Reds' success. Beckham and Giggs captained their country, while Butt, Davies, Gillespie, the Neville brothers, Savage and Scholes all became international footballers.

When trying to assess the significance of this group, Chris Casper puts it this way. What would have happened if United hadn't had these players? How would the club have been able to buy others to fill their positions? Indeed, where were there players of similar ability anywhere else? Not only that, but they brought with them a fantastic attitude to the game, and yet remained down-to-earth characters, despite all their fame and success. Raphael Burke makes the comparison with continental clubs such as Ajax and Barcelona, who have similar traditions of bringing players through. In each case, the youngsters know the club and what it stands for – 'they're not scared of the expectations'. Sometimes players brought in from outside struggle to cope with the change in environment. Savage assesses it another way: 'That youth team was probably worth £401 million – I was the million!'

Astonishingly, so long after the Class of 92 first served notice of their potential, they continue to have an impact at the very top level. Two of that group are still playing for United, as they have done some 1,600 times to date, scoring more than 300 goals for the Reds. Even when they do finally call it a day, the standards of professionalism, determination and ambition they have set for so long have made these attributes become a part of the club's DNA. Working with Sir Alex Ferguson, they have created United's insatiable appetite for success, a world where there is never any room for complacency. They have been at the heart of an unprecedented period of dominance for one club. It has been just as big a change as when Matt Busby reinvented United in the post-war era as an attacking, adventurous footballing side that gave youth its opportunity. The legacy of the Class of 92 will surely live on at United forever.

Or maybe it will eventually be surpassed. The manager certainly hopes so: 'It was not a one-off. It is going to happen again ... If Academy system changes to what it should be, then we are capable of doing it.' Perhaps it is with those words from Sir Alex – revealing his continuing drive to do better every day – that we see where the manager and his long-serving players come together to show the way forward. The Class of 92 have set a challenge to future generations to do even better. What more could a United fan want than to see that happen?

Appendix

Appearances/Goals for Manchester United by the Class of 92
(to 10 April 2012)

Player	Debut	Competition	Appearances	Goals
David Beckham	23/09/92	League Cup	394	85
Nicky Butt	21/11/92	Premier League	387	26
Chris Casper	05/10/94	League Cup	7	0
Simon Davies	21/09/94	League Cup	20	1
Ryan Giggs	02/03/91	Division One	906	163
Keith Gillespie	05/01/93	FA Cup	14	2
Colin McKee	08/05/94	Premier League	1	0
Gary Neville	16/09/92	UEFA Cup	602	7
John O'Kane	21/09/94	League Cup	7	0
Kevin Pilkington	19/11/94	Premier League	8	0
Joe Roberts	n/a		-	-
Robbie Savage	n/a		-	-
George Switzer	n/a		-	-
Lennie Taylor	n/a		-	-
Ben Thornley	26/02/94	Premier League	14	0

Those who did not play in the final:

Player	Debut	Competition	Appearances	Goals
Raphael Burke	n/a		-	-
Mark Gordon	n/a		-	-
Phil Neville	28/01/95	FA Cup	386	8
Andy Noone	n/a		-	-
Paul Scholes	21/09/94	League Cup	692	153
Total			**3438**	**445**

Class of 92

UK League Appearances/Goals in Career by the Class of 92
(to 10 April 2012)

Player	Clubs	Appearances	Goals
David Beckham	Manchester U	265	62
Raphael Burke	n/a	-	-
Nicky Butt	Manchester U, Newcastle U, Birmingham C	428	29
Chris Casper	Manchester U, Bournemouth, Swindon T, Reading	74	2
Simon Davies	Manchester U, Exeter C, Huddersfield T, Luton T, Macclesfield T, Rochdale	102	6
Ryan Giggs	Manchester U	635	112
Keith Gillespie	Manchester U, Wigan A, Newcastle U, Blackburn R, Leicester C, Sheffield U, Charlton A, Bradford C	396	27
Mark Gordon	n/a	-	-
Colin McKee	Manchester U, Bury, Kilmarnock, Partick Thistle, Falkirk, Queen of the South, Ross Co, Stirling A, Queens Park	96	12
Gary Neville	Manchester U	400	5
Phil Neville	Manchester U, Everton	484	8
Andy Noone	n/a	-	-
John O'Kane	Manchester U, Bury, Bradford C, Everton, Burnley, Bolton W, Blackpool	134	9
Kevin Pilkington	Manchester U, Rochdale, Rotherham U, Port Vale, Mansfield T, Notts Co	360	0
Joe Roberts	n/a	-	-
Robbie Savage	Crewe Alex, Leicester C, Birmingham C, Blackburn R, Derby Co, Brighton	537	37
Paul Scholes	Manchester United	478	105
George Switzer	Darlington	14	0
Lennie Taylor	n/a	-	-
Ben Thornley	Manchester U, Stockport C, Huddersfield T, Aberdeen, Blackpool, Bury	171	11
Total		**4574**	**425**

Appendix

Major Honours Won by the Class of 92 (to 10 April 2012)

Player	Club	Honours
David Beckham	Manchester United	6 PL, 2 FAC, 1 CL
	Real Madrid	1 La Liga
	LA Galaxy	1 MLS Cup
Nicky Butt	Manchester United	6 PL, 3 FAC, 1 CL
Ryan Giggs	Manchester United	12 PL, 4 FAC, 3 LC, 2 CL
Gary Neville	Manchester United	8 PL, 3 FAC, 2 LC, 1 CL
Phil Neville	Manchester United	6 PL, 2 FAC
Robbie Savage	Leicester City	1 LC
Paul Scholes	Manchester United	10 PL, 3 FAC, 2 LC, 1 CL

International Appearances/Goals by the Class of 92

Player	Debut	Country	Appearances	Goals
David Beckham	01/09/96	England	115	16
Nicky Butt	29/03/97	England	39	0
Simon Davies	24/04/96	Wales	1	0
Ryan Giggs	16/10/91	Wales	64	12
Keith Gillespie	07/09/94	Northern Ireland	86	2
Gary Neville	03/06/95	England	85	0
Phil Neville	23/05/96	England	59	0
Robbie Savage	15/11/95	Wales	39	2
Paul Scholes	24/05/97	England	66	14
Total			**554**	**46**

Bibliography

Beckham, David, *My Side* (Collins Willow, 2003)

Biddiscombe, Ross, *The Official Encyclopedia of Manchester United* (Simon & Schuster, 2011)

Endlar, Andrew, *Manchester United: The Complete Record* (Orion, 2008)

Ferguson, Alex, *Managing My Life* (Hodder & Stoughton, 1999)

Giggs, Ryan, *Giggs: The Autobiography* (Michael Joseph, 2005)

Harrison, Eric, *The View from the Dugout* (Parrs Wood Press, 2001)

Marshall, Ian, *The Official Manchester United Book of Facts and Figures* (Simon & Schuster, 2011)

Murphy, Alex, *The Official Illustrated History of Manchester United* (Simon & Schuster, 2010)

Neville, Gary, *Red: My Autobiography* (Bantam Press, 2011)

Rollin, Jack, and Glenda Rollin, *Rothmans/Sky Sports Football Yearbook* (Headline, various editions)

Savage, Robbie, *Savage! The Robbie Savage Autobiography* (Mainstream, 2011)

Scholes, Paul, *Scholes: My Story* (Simon & Schuster, 2011)
Schindler, Colin, *George Best and 21 Others* (Headline, 2004)
Whelan, Tony, *The Birth of the Babes* (Empire Publications, 2005)
White, John D.T., *Irish Devils* (Simon & Schuster, 2011)

As well as the above books, I also used the club's excellent official statistics website, www.stretfordend.co.uk and many contemporary editions of *Manchester United*, the official club magazine, and the *Manchester Evening News*.

Acknowledgements

This book could not have been written without the help of many people, and I would like to thank the following for their assistance:

At Manchester United: Steve Bartram, who managed to speak to one or two of those I could not about the Class of 92 and helped check through my text; Paul Thomas and James White, for all their help and support in putting me in touch with the players, and for their input on the manuscript; and Museum Curator Mark Wylie for his helpful advice and encouragement. Although not part of the club itself, David Meek knows it as well as almost anyone, and was a great source of advice and help.

At the Football Association, my thanks go to David Barbour for his help in clarifying how the FA Youth Cup was inaugurated.

I was able to speak to several of the Crystal Palace side who met United in the final, largely thanks to the help of Alan Edwards and John Lawrence (font of all knowledge relating to Dulwich Hamlet). From that side who came up against the Class of 92, my thanks to Sean Daly, Jimmy Glass, Niall

Thompson and Grant Watts for their memories of those days.

From the Class of 92 itself, all the members of the squad contributed in one way or another to this project, but I would particularly like to thank those who took the time to speak to me in depth: Raphael Burke, Eric Harrison, Kevin Pilkington, Joe Roberts, George Switzer, Lennie Taylor and Ben Thornley.

At Simon & Schuster, I would like to thank Ian Chapman, Kerr Macrae and Rhea Halford for giving me the opportunity to tell this wonderful story and for their patience, support and understanding.

Finally, I would like to thank my wife, Sugra, and our two daughters, Kiri and Sophia, for allowing me to spend so much time working on this book.